Letters from Swansea

LETTERS FROM SWANSEA

J. E. ROSS

CHRISTOPHER DAVIES
SWANSEA AND LLANDYBIE

First published in mcmlxix
by Christopher Davies (Publishers) Limited
Swansea and Llandybie
Printed in Wales
by Merlin Press
Llandybie

FOREWORD

This collection of excerpts from works spanning almost eight hundred years reveals not only the changing use of language by a succession of interesting people but also the story of Swansea as it passed from rural beauty, through industrial prosperity, decay, and partial destruction to the present day.

I wish to thank all who helped in the compilation of this book, especially Mary Janes, David Bevan and Mati Rees.

J. E. Ross

CONTENTS

ILLUSTRATIONS

1

THE DEATH OF HOWEL AP GORONWY 1108

The last Welsh Lord of Gower

Then the Normans who were in the Castle of Ridcors and other castles thereabouts, seeing they could not have the upper hand of Howel ap Grono in open fight, fell to their accustomed practice of treason, and so obtained their purpose in this manner: There was one Gwgan ap Meyric who had nursed a son of Howel ap Grono, and therefore very well trusted and beloved of him as the Custome of Wales is: This Traitor being corrupted by the Normans procured his Master's death, inviting him one night to his house to make merry whither he willingly came. Then Gwgan gave notice to the garrisons of the Castles, who in the dawning of the day entred the Town, and coming about the house, gave a great shout, which awakened Howel, who couragously leaped out of his bed and sought his weapons, but the Traitor Gwgan had conveyed them away while he was asleep: Then he called for his men, but they had all fled to save their lives; and as he would have gotten away, he was taken by Gwgan and his company and strangled, which cut off his head and brought it to the castle of Ridcors; and this traiterous murder of the King's Lieutenant was left unpunished; for whatever fault the Normans committed was alwaies winked at; and if Welshmen did never so little to offend the laws of the King, it was thought a most heinous and unpardonable crime, which was the cause that afterward they rebelled against the King who sought nothing but utter destruction.

1. Enderbie, Percy: Cambria Triumphans, 1661. p. 225

GIRALDUS CAMBRENSIS IN SWANSEA 1188

Entering the province of Goer, we spent the night at the Castle of Sweynsei, which in Welsh is called Abertawe, or the fall of the river Tawe into the sea.

The next morning, the people being assembled after mass, and many having been induced to take the Cross, an aged man of that district, named Cador, thus addressed the Archbishop:

'My Lord, if I now enjoyed my former strength, and the vigour of youth, no alms should ransom me, no desire of inactivity restrain me, from engaging in the laudable undertaking you preach; but since my weak age and the injuries of time deprive me of this desirable benefit (for approaching years bring with them many comforts, which those that are passed take away) if I cannot, owing to the infirmity of my body, attain a full merit, yet suffer me, by giving a tenth of all I possess to attain a half.'

Then falling down at the feet of the Archbishop, he deposited in his hands, for the service of the Cross, the tenth of his estate, weeping bitterly and intreating from him the remission of one half of the enjoined penance. After a short time he returned and continued thus:

'My Lord, if the will directs the action and is itself, for the most part, considered as the act, and as I have a full and firm inclination to undertake this journey, I request a remission of the remaining part of the penance, and in addition to my former gift, I will equal the sum from the residue of tenths.'

The Archbishop, smiling at his devout ingenuity, embraced him with admiration!

Nature hath given not only to the highest, but also to the inferior, classes of this nation, a boldness and confidence in speaking and answering, even in the presence of their princes and chieftains. The Britons . . . transplanted from the hot and parched regions of Dardania into these more temperate districts, still retain their brown complexion and that natural warmth of temper from which their confidence is derived. The heads of different families, in order to excite the laughter of their guests, and gain credit by their sayings, make use of great facetiousness in their conversation; at one time uttering their jokes in a bright easy manner, at another time, under guise of equivocation, passing the severest censures. A person wishing to hint at the avaricious disposition of the mistress of a house said, 'I only find fault with our hostess for putting too little butter to her salt.'

These people, being of a sharp and acute intellect and gifted with a rich and powerful understanding, excel in whatever studies they pursue, and are more quick and cunning than the inhabitants of a western clime. Their musical instruments charm and delight the ear with their sweetness. In their musical concerts they do not sing in unison like the inhabitants of other countries, but in many parts, so that in a company of singers, you will hear as many different parts and voices as there are performers, who all at length unite, with organic melody, in one consonance, and the soft sweetness of B flat. The practice is now so firmly rooted in them that it is unusual to hear a simple melody well sung; and what is still more wonderful, the children, even from their infancy sing in the same manner.

2. Giraldus Cambrensis: The Itinerary through Wales, J. M. Dent & Sons, 1908. pp. 67-8, 171-5.
Giraldus, also known as Gerald of Wales and Gerald de Barri. Born at Manorbier Castle, youngest son of the Norman castellan, William de Barri. Grandson of Nest. Educated in Paris. In 1175 appointed Archdeacon of Brecon. Entered Royal service. In 1188 toured Wales with the Archbishop of Canterbury, Baldwin, to raise soldiers for the third Crusade. Itinerarium Cambriae (1191).

THE DISPUTE OVER GOWER

In xiii yere of Edward felle a grete distauns betwix many lords: and this was the cause. There was a knyte thei cleped Sir William Brews, a gret wastoure of good, whech had a baronye in the March of Wales; thei clepe it Gowere Londis. He seld this baronie to dyvers lordis, and took his mony. First to Humphrey Brown, erl of Herford; next seld he the same to to lordis, both hite Roger and eke Mortimer; the on was uncle on the othir cousin. Thanne was there anothir lord thei cleped Sere Jon Mounbray. He had wedded the doutyr of this William Brews whech was sole eyir onto him: wherfor he chalenged this lond be heritage. Last of alle, and werst, Hugo Spenser the younger, he desired these londes and boute hem; and because he was the Kyngis Chambirleyn, that sale was moost alowed and approved; in so mech that he entered the londis. At this dede the othir lordes had gret indignacion. The erl of Hereforth, which was the first biere, complayned on to Thomas of Lancastir; and they gadered many barones to lyve and deye on thoo tretoures that were about the Kyng, specialy on the too Spenseris, the fadir and the son, for they reuled the Kyng as thei wold; and there was no barn ne bischop schuld stand in the Kyngis grace, but if they wolde.

3. Capgrave, John: Chronicle of England. Ed: Hingeston, F. C., pp. 186-7
Capgrave, John. 1394-1464. D.D. Oxford.
Born at Lynn, Norfolk.
Lecturer in theology.
Wrote mainly in Latin.
In English, A Chronicle of England from the Creation to 1417.

EDWARD II's FLIGHT TO WALES 1326

From the sea they made their way towards Wales to the Castle of Noeth, wandering hither and thither like daft persons. Wonderful it was that, while the land on all sides was tranquil, free from bloodshed and tumult, the King fled deliberately from London towards West Wales, as fast as his feet could carry him.

4. Henry of Knighton.

—o—

The King was at Margam on Nov. 3rd and 4th. On the 3rd he granted letters of protection for one year to John Joseph, master of the King's ship called Godyer (Goodyer) of Kaerdif, and seven mariners of the same ship.

While at Neath, the King made appeals to the men of Gower to come to his aid, but, with the men of Glamorgan they had a long quarrel to settle with Hugh (le Despenser), and, as a people they were not too ready at any time to co-operate with the men of Glamorgan.

Did the King, who, at Margam, made arrangements about the Cardiff ship 'Goodyer' and the protection of the coast, set out once more on a sea-trip, to be driven back to Neath again, to suit the chroniclers? Or, what is of more local interest, did he visit Swansea Castle? We have seen that he had ordered that the town should be provisioned and defended.

That the King's papers fell as a booty into the hands of common soldiers, or rebels, or got astray, is partly evinced by the belated discovery in Swansea of an important document, in the second quarter of the last century.

There is preserved in a frame, under glass, in the Museum of the Royal Institution of South Wales, at Swansea, the original of the Marriage Contract of King Edward II and Isabella of France.

Mr. R. W. Banks, in his account of the find in the Archaeologia Cambrensis, 5th ser. iv. 53-7, takes for granted that the King made a short stay at Swansea. 'There can be little doubt that the King, in his flight from London, carried it with him; and that in his anxiety to escape he left it behind in the castle, with whatever else he could not readily carry away with him.

The marriage contract was either overlooked or left behind. Into whose custody it fell, or continued to be, until the present century, we have no account. All that is known is that rather more than fifty years ago a poor patient of the late Dr. Nicholl, of Swansea, unable to give him a pecuniary remuneration for his services, begged his acceptance of a small box containing old deeds and papers, among which was the marriage contract. Soon after the opening of the Royal Institution in 1835, Dr. Nicholl, at the instance of Colonel Francis, presented it to the Museum.'

5. Griffith, Rev. J.: Western Mail, Cardiff, 1904. pp. 194, 197, 199, 200.

LEWIS GLYN COTHI IN GOWER

Yfory awn I Fro Ŵyr,
Ni aethom yno neithiwr;
Doe hwyliaw, da wehelyth

Trenydd; a pheunydd; a phyth
Heddyw'dd af, Sion ap Dafydd,
Heno i'w dai yn y dydd.
Impyn yw'n mhob pen i ŵyr,
A'i gred ieuanc hyd awyr!
A gwinllan deg yn llawn dail
Ym Mawd lle mae ei adail.

6. Gwaith Lewis Glyn Cothi. Ed. Jones, E.D., Gwasg Prifysgol Cymru, 1953; p. 191.
Lewis Glyn Cothi or Llewelyn y Glyn. fl. 1447-86.
One of the greatest itinerant Welsh bards.
Outlawed after the Battle of Mortimer's Cross, he was invited to sing by his Yorkist enemies.
He stayed for some time at Kilvey, Swansea.

LELAND IN NEATH SWANSEA AND GOWER

Glade (Gwlad) is in the Walsch a countery or a land. And this province or cuntery is often caulled Morganhog. I take Moregan to have the name of More, that is to say the se, onto the shore whereof it lyeth. The Kefinnithes (confinia) of Glamorgan ly thus:—

Remny is the marche on the est side of it. Cremline a little broke, is the march of the west part of it. The severne se boundith it from the mouth of Remny to the mouth of Cremlin. The rootes of the Blake Mountein marchith it by northe. From Pont Remny to the forde of Cremlin brooke, a mile from Swansey, is the nerest way a 23 miles . . This way be many hilles (woods good plentye) about the ryvers sides, but few villages or corne except in a few small valleys.

The mountains have some redde dere, kiddes plenty, oxen and sheep . . . From the mouth of the Avon to the mouth of Neth Ryver is about a ii miles and a half, al by low shore shokid with Severn sandes and some morisch groundes. The litle toun and castelle of Neth stondith a 4 miles from the mouth of Neth, and the toun and castle stondith on est ripe of Neth. On west ripe a little lower then the toun of Neth was the Abbay of Nethe.

On nother side of Nethe from the mouth thus far is any very

good soile. Good pasture there is in sum places and woodde, about Neth. Ther be colles half a mile above the toune of Nethe in a more, and again a little beneth the toun, almost in ripa. There cummith up shippelettes almost onto the town of Neth from the Severn. Botes cum to the very bridge of tymbre that is sumwhat lower on the water then the toun. At the very mouth of Nethe on the est side of it is a little village of 3 or 4 housis caullid Britanne Fery to pass to Swansey and Penbrokeshire.

GOWERLAND.

The olde castel of Swineseye was builded or repairid by the Normans and destroied by Luelen, prince of Wales that maryed King Johns dowghter. And it stoode by the bisshop of St. Davids castel that now is there. A iii miles from Swineseye communely cawillid in englisch, Swansey, at the rode mowth of Tawe was a castel cawllid Est Wilthlunarde, otherwise Ostermuth, and of sum Mummess. Swansey is a market town and chief place of Gowerland. Almost in the middes of Gowerland a v miles from Suansey is the Castel of Guible that longid to the Delamers. Penrise Castel standith a iii miles from Suansey in the forest of Penrise. Lochor castel standith on the hither side of Lochor river in the lordship of Gower.

7. Leland, John: The Itinerary in Wales, Ed; Smith, L.T., George Bell & Sons, London, 1906. pp. 15, 16, 30, 127, 153-6.

Leland, John. c. 1506-1552.
Born in London: studied at Oxford and Paris.
King's Antiquary: travelled in search of manuscripts, etc. after dissolution of monasteries.
Acquired many for Henry VIII.

INQUEST ON LADY ANNE MANSEL AT OXWICH

Inquest on the body of Mrs Anne Manxel, widow, January 3rd and 4th and 5th of Philip and Mary, 1557. Inquisition indented taken at Oxwich in the county aforesaid, the 3rd of January, in the year of the reigns of Philip and Mary, by the

Grace of God, King and Queen of England, Spain, France, and both Sicilies, Jerusalem and Ireland, defenders of the faith, Archduke of Austria, Duke of Burgandy, Milan and Brabant,, Count of Hapsburg, Flanders, and Tyrol, the 4th and 5th, before Thomas ap Howell, alias David Thomas ap Howell, a coroner of our Lord and Lady, the King and Queen, in the county aforesaid, upon the view of the body of Anne Manxell, late of Llandewy, in the county aforesaid, widow, at Oxwich aforesaid, in the county aforesaid, dead killed and slain: by the oaths of
Willaim ap Henry, gent.,
William Llewellyn ap John, gent.,
Hopkin John, gent.,
John ap Rice ap Thomas, gent.,
Richard ap Owen, gent.,
William Hopkins, gent.,
Jenkyn Thomas ap John, gent.,
Richard ap John David ap Morgan, gent.,
Morgan ap William, gent.,
Jenkyn ap Jenkyn ap Jenkyn, gent.,
Hopkin Thomas Phelip, yeoman,
Thomas Jankyn,
John Edwarde,
Nicholas David,
William Bennett,
Thomas Walter,
Thomas Griffith,
Richard Melyn,
and Rice ap Howell David,
who say upon their oaths, that whereas the aforesaid Anne Manxell, the 28th Day of December, in the years of our now Lord and Lady the King and Queen Philip and Mary, the 4th and 5th abovesaid, about nine o'clock before noon of the same day, was in the peace of God and our Lord and Lady, the King and Queen Philip and Mary, at Oxwiche aforesaid, in the county aforesaid, in the capital messuage of Rice Maunxell, alias Sir Rice Maunxell, Esquire, and other servants of the said Anne, then and there being. Thither approached and came, on the day and years last before mentioned,
Watkyn John ap Watkyn, late of Swansey in the county aforesaid,

yeoman, alias Watkyn John ap Watkyn, late of Swansey in the county aforesaid servingman,
George Herbert, late of Swansey, in the county aforesaid Knight, alias George Herbert,
William Herbert, late of London gent., alias Willim Herbert, late of Chepstow, in the county of Monmouth gent.,
John ap John Thomas David ap Howel, late of Margam, in the county aforesaid, gent.,
Henry Watkyn, late of Swansey, in the county aforesaid, gent.,
Hugh David ap Jenkyn, late of Swansey, in the county aforesaid, yeoman,
John Richard ap Jenkyn ap Jankyn, late of Lanmaes, in the county aforesaid, yeoman,
John ap John David, late of Lanmaes in the county aforesaid yeoman, alias John ap John Rice Weith, late of Lanmaes in the county aforesaid, yeoman,
Lodwick Holand, late of Swansey in the county aforesaid, taylor, alias Lodwick Roland, in the county aforesaid, yeoman,
Thomas Grayle, in the county aforesaid, yeoman,
Roger Jankyn, in the county aforesaid, merchant,
Watkyn ap Harry, late of Swansey in the county aforesaid, yeoman, and Thomas Johns, late of St. Andrews, in the county aforesaid, gent., with the intention of hurting the aforesaid Edward Manxell . . . with force of arms, to wit, with swords, staves and knives, then at Oxwich made an assault and the aforesaid Watkyn John ap Watkyn held in his right hand a stone of no great bigness which . . . with great force and power, he threw at the said Anne Manxell and with that stone, upon the forehead of the said Anne, struck and gave a certain mortal wound in the forehead aforesaid, of the breadth of two thumbs and the depth even to the brain, of which mortal wound, the said Anne Maunxell at Oxwich aforesaid, from the 28th day of December to the 1st day of January then following, languished; on which 1st day of January the same Anne Maunxell died of the aforesaid wound.

IN CAMERA STELLA.

Upon deliberate hearing of the matter in variaunce between Sir Rice Maunxell, Knight, and Edward Maunxell, his sonne, complaynants, and Sir George Herbert, Knight, and others, his servants and Retynue, Deffendaunts ffor and concerning dyvers and sondrye Ryotts forces batries and other misdemeanours . . . Riottous and forcyble entrye into the howse of one Sir Richard Cossyn, clerke . . . and the taking awaye from thence six peeces of fygges and one horne of gunne powder of the goods of the said Sir Rice Maunxell seased of certen Frenchmen in tyme of warre. And also for and concerninge another Riottous and forcyble entrye the same daye into the castell and mansion howse of the said Sir Rice Maunxell and the ryottouse spoyling, Ryfeling and taking awaye of three Frenchmen and a flemmyng . . .

And finally for and concerning another riottous and haynous assaulte and affraye . . . at the castell or Mansion howse of the said Sir Rice Maunxell by the said Sir George Herbert in his prop' p'sone . . against the aforesaid Edward Maunxell standing and being with others in Godes peace and the King and Queen in the gate of the said howse for the defence and safe kepynge of the said howse and his father's goods therein which the said Sir George p'sumed to enter and take awaye. In which Riott force and affraye the said Edward Maunxell was wounded and hurte. And one Anne Maunxell, his aunte, then and ther deadly wounded by the throwing of a stone . . And for that the said Sir George Herbert hath in the'nd of the hering of the said matter openly confessed all the said Ryottes it is therefore this present daye being the 13th of Maye ordered and decreed by this hon'able Courte of the Star Chamber that the said Sir George Herbert and such of his s'unts and retynue as are now p'sent for the said offences shall be committed to the fleete and there to Remayne tyll further order be taken . . . And also that the said S. George Harbet and his s'unts and retynue shall paye to our said souereynes such fynes . . . as by this court shall be adjudged assessed and deliver and repaye . . . such prisoners, merchandises goods and cattells or as much money . . . as by order of this courte shall be adjudged and awarded.

8. Davies, J. D., Historical Notices of West Gower, part iv. pp. 163-195.
Davies, Rev, John David. 1831-1911.
Son of John Davies, rector of Reynoldston, born at Oxwich Parsonage: entered Trinity College, Dublin, as a Rossall scholar: graduated 1855: M.A. 1859:
assistant curate of Nicholaston:

rector of Llanmadoc 1860: Cheriton 1867:
restored both churches:
hobbies — wood carving and research:
published history of Gower in 4 volumes (1877-94):
buried at Cheriton Church.

A VISIT TO THE REV. J. D. DAVIES

Tuesday 16 April: 1871.

After breakfast we set out to drive to Llanmadoc, over high commons, then through pretty lanes, catching glimpses of the Carmarthenshire coast, Pembrey, Burry Port, and the smoke of Llanelly, across the sands and blue water of the arm of Carmarthen Bay called the Bury River.

A sharp pull up and steep hill brought us to Llanmadoc on the brow of a windy bare hill looking out on Carmarthen Bay. Westhorp and Mrs. Westhorp went into the bare unfinished ugly barrack of a Rectory while I minded Bob and the wagonette. Presently they came out with the Vicar, Mr Davies, who looked like a Roman priest, close shaven and shorn, dressed in seedy black, a long coat and broad shovel hat.

He took us into the Churchyard, but let us find our own way into the Church which was beautifully finished and adorned but fitted up in high ritualistic style. The Vicar said that when he came to the place the Church was meaner than the meanest hovel in the village.

The Vicar invited us to join him at his luncheon to which we added the contents of our picnic basket. He had a very good pie to which we did justice for we were all very hungry with the sea air. We were waited on by a tall clean old women with a severe and full cap border who waits on Mr Davies and is so clean that she washes the kitchen four times a day. She used to wash her master's bedroom floor as often till he caught a cold which frightened her and she desisted.

We suggested that she might be of Flemish blood which would account for her cleanliness. The idea had never occurred to Mr Davies and he was much struck by it. The house was thoroughly untidy and bachelorlike and full of quaint odds and ends. The rigging of a boat stood in the hall for the Vicar is a great sailor and sails Carmarthen Bay in a boat built by himself. A quantity of pretty wood fretwork and carved work also stood about in the hall and rooms, and miniature bookcases and cabinets for drawing-room tables made by himself and sold for the benefit of Cheriton Church Restoration Fund. He is very clever and can turn his hand to anything. Besides which he seemed to me an uncommonly kind good fellow, a truly simple-minded single-hearted man.

The Vicar showed us what he called his newest toy-machine almost like a sewing-machine—for sewing out the pattern in his wood carving. He promised to make me a little 10/- bookcase.

9. Kilvert, Rev, Francis: Diary of. Ed: Plomer, William. Jonathon Cape. vol. 2. p. 183.
Kilvert, Rev. F. 1840-79.
Diary now considered an important social historical record of late 19*c.* (1870-9):
regular visitor to Ilston Rectory:
Vicar of Bredwardine.

THE BILAND OF GOWER

Beyond this river Neath, whatsoever lieth betweene it and the river Loghor, which boundeth this shire in the West, wee call Gower: the Britans and Ninnius, Guhir: wherin, as he saith, the sonnes Keian the Scot planted themselves, and tooke up a large room, untill by Cuneda a British Lord they were driven out. In the reigne of Henrie the first, Henrie Earle of Warwick wonne it from the Welsh, but by a conveiance and composition, passed between William Earle of Warwick and King Henrie the second, it came to the crowne. Afterward King John gave it to William Breos who had taken Arthur E. of Britaine prisoner, to be held by service of one knight for all service: and his heires successively held it not without troubles unto King Edward the Seconds daies: for then, William Breos, when he had alienated and sold this inheritance to many, and in the end by mocking and disappointing all others, set Hugh Spencer in possession thereof, to curry favour with the King. And this was one cause, among other things, that the Nobles hated the Spensers so deadly, and rashly shooke off their allegiance to the King. Howbeit this Gower came to the

Mowbraies by and heirs of Breos. This is now divided into the East part and the West. In the East part Swineseye, is of great account, a toune so called by the Englishmen, of Sea-wine: but the Britans Aber-taw. Taw of the river Taw running by it; which the foresaid Henry, Earle of Warwick fortified. But there is a town farre more ancient than this by the river Loghor, which Antonine the Emperor called Leucarum, and we, by the whole name, Loghor. Where a little after the death of King Henrie the First, owel, ap Meredic, invading the Englishmen on a sodaine, with a powre of the mountainers slew divers men of quality and good account. Beneath this lieth West Gower, and by reason of two armes of the sea winding in, on either side, it becommeth a Biland more memorable for the fruitfulnesse, than the townes in it, and in some times past of great name, in regard to Kined canonized a Saint, who lived heere a solitarie life: of whom if you desire to know more read, our country man Capgrave who hath set out his miracle with great commendation.

10. Camden, William (1551-1623) Britain; a Chorographical Description of the most flourishing Kingdomes. Tr: Holland, Philemon; Bishop and Norton, 1610, p. 646. First published in Latin in 1586.

WALLOGRAPHY

Having had the honour to be employ'd in a negotiation between an English gentleman and the ancient Britons, I was not only upon the borders, and (as it were) the limb of Wales, but have travelled through the very bowels of the countryside. In which journey there did salute me so many occurrences worthy of observation, that I could not forbear a description of them, and presenting you with (as I may say) the Wallography of my voyage. I make bold to imitate one Alexander of Greece, who still, as he went dragooning about the world, described the wandering and (as it were) the Tom Coriatism of his expeditions; only in this I shall differ from him; whereas he gave only a bare image and pourtraiture of the country, I shall draw the character of the inhabitants, and shall not only express in a map or table the mere picture of the place and tell you that here stands one town, and twenty miles off stands another; but my design is to give you a narrative of what I observed concerning the nature of the soil, and of the inhabitants, their original, persons, diet, apparel, language, laws, customs, policy, etc. .

But what need I go as far as Macedonia for a pattern, seeing we have so many precedents at home? For one tells us in folio, that he hath been in Constantinople; another that he hath been at Vienna; a third, that he hath been in Spain, and why may I not tell the world in doudecimo, that I have been in Wales?

I do not know that any traveller, jogging along the same road, hath given the same descriptions which I here present you with; so that my remarks are spick and span new, and if they are ridiculous, they are not unlike the persons upon whom they are written. For the Welsh are a pretty odd sort of mortals, and I hope I have given you a pretty odd character of them, and so think I am pretty even with them for their oddness. A Taphy is observed to be a trickish animal, that hath a vein of Jackpuddinism running through all his actions, and therefore I thought it not improper to sprinkle here and there somewhat of the blue-jacket and to merry-andrew my progress a little farther, as I went, with jocund observations, that the history might be agreeable to the matter it treats of. So that if a Welshman is a jest, as all the world accounts him a living pun, a walking conundrum, and a breathing witticism, then I have made one joke upon another.

Now for the conclusion of all; if there are any good things in Wales, the enjoyment thereof is worth wishing you, I pray heaven to crown you with the fruition of them: but possibly it may be a province not much crowded with blessings; may you therefore flourish in the affluence of good English mercies; may you always possess good English riches health and honours, and all other happiness and prosperities of our own nation.

I am, (worthy sir!)

Your very humble servant.

We perceived their herds to be frequently mingled with little palfries, a stunted sort of horses, diminutive brutes, shavals in shorthand. They are lower in stature than an ass, but much swifter in foot, and very strong; as it appears from their burdens which are often-times the fortune and substance of a whole family; for when a mortal breaks, he mounts all he hath in a Welsh nag, and travels under the character of a Scotch pedlar. We chanc'd to see a team of this small cattle, a rare spectacle, being (as we suppos'd) the least that was ever heard of, unless that which was harness'd in Venus's chariot, which was a team of doves. The British steeds are so brisk and mercurial, that the people would persuade us that a Taphy on a tit, would outstrip in travel an Arabian on a dromedary; a thing most incredible, though the pricking up their ears, and the flicking up their tails, is an argument of their mettle, and may give some colour and ground for this assertion.

That which we admired most of all amongst them was the virginity of their language, not deflower'd by the mixture of any other dialect; the purity of Latin was debauch'd by the vandals, and was hunn'd into corruption by that barbarous people; but the sincerity of the British remains inviolable. 'Tis a tongue (it seems) not made for every mouth; as appears by an instance of one of our company, who having got a Welsh polysyllable into his throat was almost choak'd with consonants, had we not, by clapping him on the back, made him disgorge a guttural or two, and so sav'd him. They usually liquify the most rugged mutes, and soften 'em by pronunciation; melting the word tug into tudge, as is clear from this distich:

> Still did he tudge her ear
> In praise of the tirteen seer.

i.e., did tug her souses with elogiums of hur country.

Whether the Welsh tongue be a splinter of that universal one that was shatter'd at Babel, we have some reason to doubt in regard 'tis unlike the dialects that were crumbled there; however whether it be kin or no to other country speeches, it matters not; but this we are assur'd of, it is near and dear to the folk that utter it, who are so passionately fond of it, that they will scarce admit another into the embraces of their lips, which sputter forth a kind of loathing of our English language; wherein, if a question be ask'd them, they will, with somewhat of disdain and choler, make answer, Dim Saissonick, i.e., no English. Their native gibberish is usually prattled throughout the whole Taphydome, except in thir market towns, whose inhabitants being a little raised, and (as it were) puff'd up into bubbles above the ordinary scum, do begin to despise it. Some of these being elevated above the common level, and perhaps refin'd into the quality of having two suits, are apt to fancy themselves above their tongue, and, when in their other cloaths, are quite asham'd on't. 'Tis usually cashiered out of gentlemen's houses, there being scarcely to be heard even one single Welsh tone in many families; their children are instructed in the Anglican idiom, and their schools are pedagogu'd with professors of the same; so that (if the stars prove lucky) there may be some glimmering hopes that British lingua may be quite extinct and may be English'd out of Wales, as Latin was barbarously Goth'd out of Italy.

11. Richards, William: Wallography. Obadiah Blagrave, 1682.
Richards, William. 1643-1705.
Born at Helmdon Rectory, Northants.
Trinity College, Oxford.
Lecturer at St. Andrews, Newcastle on Tyne. 1689.
Travelled to Wales on business for a friend. 1673.
Wallography published under initials W.R. in 1682.
Re-published in 1709 and ascribed to Swift.
In 1753 W.R. was accused of imitating Swift, aged 15 at time of first issue.
Buried in Newcastle at St. Andrews.

BEAU NASH

The following memoir is neither calculated to enflame the reader's passions with descriptions of gallantry nor to gratify his malevolence with details of scandal. The amours of coxcombs, and the pursuits of debauchees, are destitute of novelty to attract us, as they are of variety to entertain, they still present us but the same picture we have seen a thousand times repeated. The life of Mr. Nash is incapable of supplying any entertainment of this nature to a prurient curiosity. Though it was past in the very midst of debauchery, he practised but few of these vices he was often obliged to assent to. Though he lived where gallantry was the capital pursuit, he was never known to favour it by his example, and what authority he had was set to oppose it. Instead

SOURCE OF THE TAWE — I. G. WOOD 1813

THE DESCENT OF THE TAWE — I. G. WOOD 1811

Swansea Castle and Harbour

Swansea Castle

NEATH ABBEY

OYSTERMOUTH CASTLE

Weobley Castle S. & N. Buck 1741

Penard Castle S. & N. Buck 1741

Oxwich Castle

Abertawe from Kilvey

Swansea from the West

Gathering Seaweed 1825

Wesley Chapel and Birthplace of Nash

The Tawe Ferry Rothwell

therefore of a romantic history, filled with warm pictures and fanciful adventures, the reader of the following account must rest satisfied with a genuine and candid recital compiled from the papers he left behind, and others equally authentic; a recital neither written with a spirit of satire nor panygeyric, and with scarce any other art, than that of arranging the materials in their natural order.

But though little art has been used, it is hoped that some entertainment may be collected from the life of a person so much talked of, and yet so little known as Mr. Nash. The history of a man, who for more than fifty years presided over the measures of a polite kingdom, and whose life, though without anything to surprise, was ever marked with singularity,, deserves the attention of the present age: the pains he took in pursuing pleasure, and the solemnity he assumed in adjusting trifles, may one day claim the smile of posterity. Yet his life how trifling soever it may appear to the inattentive, was not without its real advantages to the public. He was the first who diffused a desire of society, and an easiness of addressing among a whole people who were formerly censured by foreigners for a reservedness of behaviour and an awkward timidity in their first approaches. He first taught a familiar intercourse among strangers at Bath and Tunbridge, which still subsists among them. The ease and open access first acquired there our gentry brought back to the metropolis, and thus the whole kingdom by degrees became more refined by lessons originally derived from him.

It is a matter of very little importance who were the parents or what was the education of a man who owed so little of his advancement to either. He seldom boasted of family or learning, and his father's name and circumstance were so little known, that Doctor Cheyne used frequently to say, that Nash had no father.

The Duchess of Marlboro' one day rallying him in public company upon the obscurity of his birth, compared him to Gil Blas, who was ashamed of his father: No, Madam, replied Nash, I seldom mention my father in company, not because I have any reason to be ashamed of him; but because he has reason to be ashamed of me.

RULES TO BE OBSERVED AT BATH

1. That a visit of ceremony at first coming and another at going away, are all that are expected or desired, by ladies of quality and fashion — except impertinents.
2. That ladies coming to the ball appoint a time for their footmen coming to wait on them home, to prevent disturbance and inconvenience to themselves and others.
3. That gentlemen of fashion never appearing in a morning before the ladies in gowns and caps, show breeding and respect.
4. That no person take it ill that anyone goes to another's play, or breakfast, and not theirs . . . except captious by nature.
5. That no gentleman gives his tickets for the balls, to any but gentlewomen . . . N.B. unless he has none of his acquaintance.
6. That gentlemen crowding before the ladies at the ball shew ill manners; and that none do so for the future except such as respect nobody but themselves.
7. That no gentleman or lady takes it ill that another dances before them . . . except such as have no pretence to dance at all.
8. That the elder ladies and children be content with a second bench at the ball, as being past or not yet come to perfection.
9. That the younger ladies take notice how many eyes observe them. N.B. This does not extend to the Have-at-alls.
10. That all whisperers of lies and scandal be taken for their authors.
11. That all repeaters of such lies and scandal be shunn'd by all company; . . . except such as have been guilty of the same crime.

N.B. Several men of no character, old women and young ones, of refined reputation, are great authors of lies in these places, being of the sect of levellers.

12. Goldsmith, Oliver: Life of Beau Nash, Sisley's Ltd., London. pp. 5, 11, 12, 28-9.

BEAU NASH AND JOHN WESLEY

June 1739
Tues. 5.

There was a great expectation at Bath of what a noted man was to do to me there; and I was much entreated not to preach, because no one knew what might happen. By this report I also gained a much larger audience, among whom were many of the rich and great. I told them plainly, 'The Scripture had concluded them all under sin,' high and low, rich and poor, one with another. Many of them seemed to be a little surprised, and were sinking apace ino seriousness, when their champion appeared, and coming close to me, asked, 'By what authority I did these things?' I replied, 'By the authority of Jesus Christ, conveyed to me by the (now) Archbishop of Canterbury, when he laid his hands upon me and said, 'Take thou authority to preach the Gospel.' He said, 'This is contrary to Act of Parliament. This is a conventicle.' I answered, 'Sir, the conventicles mentioned in that Act (as the preamble shows) are seditious meetings; but this is not such; here is no shadow of sedition; therefore it is not contrary to that Act.' He replied, 'I say it is: and beside, your preaching frightens people out of their wits.' 'Sir, did you ever hear me preach?' 'No.' 'How then can you judge of what you never heard?' 'Sir, by common report.' 'Common report is not enough. Give me leave, Sir, to ask, is not your name Nash?' 'My name is Nash.' 'Sir, I dare not judge of you by common report. I think it is not enough to judge by.'

Here he paused awhile, and having recovered himself, said, 'I desire to know what this people comes here for?' On which one replied, 'Sir, leave him to me. Let an old woman answer him.' 'You, Mr. Nash take care of your body. We take care of our souls; and for the food of our souls we come here.' He replied not a word, but walked away.

Aug. 8.

Having promised a little journey into Wales on Monday, 21st, I set out with Joseph Jones. We reached Swansea at seven, and were met by one who conducted us to his house, and thence to a kind of castle, in which was a green court, surrounded by high, old walls. A large congregation assembled soon, and behaved with the utmost decency. A very uncommon blessing was among them, as uses to be among them that are simple of heart. The congregation was considerably more than doubled at five in the afternoon. Many gay and well-dressed persons were among them, but they were as serious as the poorest.

Mon. 28th.

I scarce ever saw such a rain in Europe, as we had for a considerable part of this morning. In one of the main streets, the water ran with a stream capable of turning a mill. However, having appointed to preach in Newton, about six miles from Swansea, I was determined not to break my word, though I supposed but few would attend: but I was mistaken. Such a number of people came together as no house in the town could contain. A barn was soon prepared: and it pleased Gd to send a gracious rain upon their hearts.

After preaching at Swansea in the evening, I met those who desired to join in a Society, and explained the nature and design of it, with which they were quite unacquainted.

Tue. 29.

I rode back to Neath, in order to put the Society there (an unlicked mass) into some form. This on Saturday, they had begged me to do; but they seemed now to have quite forgotten it. Mr. Evans, the Presbyterian Minister, had turned them upside down. They looked as if they had never seen me before; all but five or six, who were much ashamed of their brethren.

Wed. 30.

I rode to Margum. There used to be preaching here, till Lord Mansel, dying without children, left the estate to Mr. Talbot. He forbade all his tenants to ıeceive the Preachers, and so effectually put a stop to it; but he did not glory in it long. A few months after God called him home.

1763
Aug.

I preached, at seven, to one or two hundred people, many of

whom seemed full of good desires. But as there is no Society, I expect no deep or lasting work.

Mr. Evans now gave me an account, from his own knowledge, of what has made a great noise in Wales.

'It is common in the congregations attended by Mr. W. and one or two clergymen, after the preaching is over, for any one that has a mind, to give out a verse of a hymn. This they sing over and over with all their might, perhaps above thirty, yea, forty times. Meanwhile the bodies of two or three, sometimes ten or twelve are violently agitated, and they leap up and down, in all manner of postures, frequently for hours together.' I think there needs no great penetration to understand this. They are honest, upright men, who really feel the love of God in their hearts; but they have little experience, either of the ways of God, or the devices of Satan. So he serves himself of their simplicity, in order to wear them out, and to bring a discredit on the work of God.

Tue. 31 July 1764.

We set out for Glamorganshire, and rode up and down steep and stony mountains for about five hours to Larn. Having procured a pretty passage there, we went to Llansteffan-Ferry; where we were in the water. Between one and two we reached Kidwelly, having been more then seven hours on horseback, in which time we could have rode round by Carmarthen, with more ease to man and beast. I have therefore taken my leave of these ferries; considering we save no time by crossing them, (not even when we have a ready passage) and so have all the trouble, danger, and expense, clear gains. I wonder that any man of common sense, who has once made the experiment, should ever ride from Pembroke to Swansea any other way than by Carmarthen.

An honest man at Kidwelly told us there was no difficulty in riding the sands. So we rode on. In ten minutes one overtook us who used to guide persons over them. And it was well he did, or in all probability, we had been swallowed up. The whole sands are at least ten miles over, with many streams of quicksands intermixed. But our guide was thoroughly acquainted with them, and with the road on the other side. By his help, between five and six, we came well tired to Oxwych, in Gower.

Gower is a large tract of land, bounded by Brecknockshire on the north-east, the sea on the south-west, and rivers on the other sides. Here all the people talk English, and are, in general, the most plain, loving people in Wales.

Knowing they were scattered up and down, I had sent two persons on Sunday, that they might be there early on Monday, and so sent notice of my coming all over the country. But they came to Oxwych scarce a quarter of an hour before me, so that the poor people had no notice at all. Nor was there any to take us in; the person with whom the Preacher used to lodge being three miles out of town. After I had stayed a while in the street (for there was no public house) a poor woman gave me house room. Having had nothing since breakfast, I was very willing to eat or drink; but she simply told me, 'She had nothing in the house but a dram of gin.' However, I afterwards procured a dish of tea at another house and was much refreshed. About seven I preached to a little company, and again in the morning. They were all attention; so that even for the sake of this handful I did not regret my labour.

Tue. Aug. 9 1768.

I took a full view of the Castle, situate on the top of a steep hill, and commanding a various and extensive prospect, both by sea and land. The building itself is far the loftiest which I have seen in Wales. What a taste had they who removed from hence to bury themselves in that hole at Margum.

13. Wesley, John. Journal. Everyman Edition. Vol. I. p. 198.
Vol. II pp. 425-6. Vol. III. pp. 145-6, 196, 344-5.
Beau Nash 1674-1761
Master of Ceremonies at Bath, 1705.
'Through his exertions a handsome assembly rooms was built and the city generally improved. He wore an immense white hat as a sign of office, and a dress adorned with rich embroidery, and drove in a chariot with six grays, laced lackeys and French horns.'
Enc. Brit.
Oliver Goldsmith. c 1730-1774.

John Wesley, 1703-91.
15th child of the Rector of Epworth.
Educated at Charterhouse and Oxford.
Ordained deacon in 1725 and priest in 1728.
Worked at first in Bristol and London and intervening places.
Went to Ireland first in 1747; 42 visits in all.
Called at places in Gower and in Swansea on the way.
Oxwich has a Wesley Cottage still.

DANIEL DEFOE IN SWANSEA

Entering Glamorganshire we beheld the Black Mountains on the right, and all a ridge of horrid rocks and precipices between, over which, if we had not good guides, we should never have found our way; and indeed we began to repent our curiosity, in going out of the common road, as not having met anything worth the trouble; and the country looking so full of horror.

Swanzy is a seaport, and a very considerable town for trade, with a very good harbur. Here is also a very good trade for coals, and culm, which they export to all ports of Somerset, Devon, and Cornwall, and even to Ireland; so that sometimes may be seen a hundred sail of ships at a time loading coals here; which greatly enriches the country, and particularly this town; it stands on the River Twye, or Taw. 'Tis very remarkable, that most of the rivers in this county chime upon the letters T and y, as Taaf, Tawy, Tuy, Towy, and Tyvy.

There are lately mineral waters found out at Swanzy, which are reported to be of great efficacy in fluxes, and Haemorrhages of all sorts. Consumptions, if not too far gone, diabetes, palsies, rheumatisms, dropsies, and other distempers, are said to fall before these styptick and restorative waters. They certainly have very good effects in many difficult cases; but it is doing an injury to the reputation of any medicine in the world, to make it a Catholicon, ,and good for everything.

14. Defoe, Daniel. Tour through the whole island of Britain. 1745.
Daniel Defoe 1660-1731.
Declined the ministry and set up as a merchant.
Arrested for seditious libel in 1703.
Excerpt from warrant:—a middle sized man, spare, of a brown complexion, and dark-brown coloured hair, but wears a wig, a hooked nose, a sharp chin, grey eyes, and a large mole near his mouth.
Travelled extensively for the government and published his Tour in 3 volumes from 1724-7.

THE TRAGEDY OF RICHARD SAVAGE

It does not appear Johnson wrote anything in 1774 for the Gentleman's Magazine, but the preface. But he produced one work this year fully sufficient to maintain the high reputation which he had acquired. This was the life of Richard Savage; a man of whom it is difficult to speak impartially without wondering that he was for some time the intimate companion of Johnson; for his character was marked by profligacy, insolence, and ingratitude: yet, as he undoubtedly had a warm and vigorous, though unregulated mind, had seen life in all its varieties, and had been much in the company of the statesmen and wits of his time, he could communicate to Johnson an abundant supply of such materials as his philosophical curiosity most eagerly desired. It is melancholy to reflect that Johnson and Savage were sometimes in such extreme indigence that they could not pay for a lodging; so that they wandered whole nights together in the streets. He told Sir Joshua Reynolds that one night in particular when Savage and he walked round St. James's Square for want of a lodging they were not at all depressed; but in high spirits and brimful of patriotism, traversed the square for several hours; inveighed against the minister and resolved to stand by their country. I am afraid, however, that by associating with Savage, who was habituated to the dissipation and licentiousness of the town, Johnson, though his good principles remained steady, did not entirely preserve that conduct, for which, in days of greater simplicity, he was remarked by his friend, Mr Hector; but was imperceptibly led into some indulgences which occasioned much distress to his virtuous mind.

That Johnson was anxious that an authentick and favourable account of his extraordinary friend should first get possession of the publick attention is evident from a letter which he wrote in the Gentleman's Magazine for August of the year preceding publication.

Mr Urban,

As your collections show often you have owed the ornaments of your poetical pages to the correspondence of the unfortunate and ingenious Mr Savage, I doubt not but you have so much regard to his memory as to encourage my design that may have a tendency to the preservation of it from insults or calumnies; and therefore, with some degree of assurance, intreat you to inform the public, that his life will speedily be published by a person who was favoured with his confidence, and received from himself an account of most of the transactions which he proposes to mention, to the time of his retirement to Swansea in Wales. My account will be published in 8vo by Mr Roberts in Warwick Lane.

So peculiar were the Misfortunes of this Man deprived of an Estate and Title by particular Law, exposed and abandoned by a Mother, defrauded of a Fortune which his Father allotted him, he entered the World without a Friend; and though his Abilities forced themselves into Esteem and Reputation, he was never able to obtain any real Advantage and whatever Prospects arose, were always intercepted as he began to approach them.

Such were the Misfortunes, which yet he bore, not only with Decency, but with Cheerfulness; nor was his Gaiety clouded even by his last Disappointment, though he was in a short Time reduced to the lowest Degree of Distress, and often wanted both Lodging and Food.

His Distress was now publicly known, and his Friends, therefore, thought it proper to concert some Measures for his Relief; and one of them wrote a Letter to him in which he expressed Concern for the miserable Withdrawing of his Pension; and gave Hopes, that in a short Time, he should find himself supplied with a Competence without any Dependence of those little Creatures which we are pleased to call Great.

The Scheme proposed for this happy and independent Subsistence was that he should retire into Wales and receive an Allowance of Fifty Pounds a Year, to be raised by a Subscription on which he was to live privately in a cheap Place, without aspiring any more to Affluence, or having any farther Care of reputation.

This offer Mr. Savage gladly accepted, though with very different Intentions from those of his Friends, for they proposed that he should continue an Exile from London for ever, and spend all the remaining Part of his Life at Swansea: but he designed only to take the Opportunity which their Scheme offered him, of retreating for a short Time, that he might prepare his Play for the Stage, and his other Works for the Press, and then return to exhibit his Tragedy, and live upon the Profits of his Labour.

As he was ready to entertain himself with future Pleasures he had planned a Scheme of Life for the Country, of which he had no knowledge but from Pastorals and Songs. He imagined that he should be transported to Scenes of flowery Felicity, like those which one Poet has reflected to another; and had projected a perpetual Round of innocent Pleasures, of which he suspected no Interruption from Pride, Ignorance or Brutality.

With these Expectations he was so enchanted, that when he was once gently reproached by a Friend for submitting to live on a Subscription, and advised rather by an Exertion of his Abilities to support himself, he could not bear to debar himself from the Happiness which was to be found in the Calm of a Cottage, or lose the Opportunity of listening without Intermission, to the Melody of the Nightingale, which he believed was to be heard from every Bramble, and which he did not fail to mention as a very important Part of the Happiness of a Country Life.

After many Alterations and Delays, a Subscription was at length raised, which did not amount to fifty Pounds a Year, though twenty were paid by one Gentleman. (Pope)

Mr Savage, however, was satisfied, and willing to retire, and was convinced that an Allowance, though scanty, would be more than sufficient for him being now determined to commence a rigid Oeconomist, and to live according to the exact Rules of Frugality; for nothing was, in his Opinion, more contemptible than a Man, who, when he knew his Income, exceeded it . . .

Full of these salutary Resolutions, he left London in July 1739, having taken Leave with great Tenderness of his Friends, and parted from the Author of this Narrative with Tears in his Eyes. He was furnished with fifteen Guineas, and informed they would be sufficient not only for the Expence of his Journey, but of his support in Wales for some Time; and that there remained but little more of his first Collection. He promised a strict Adherence to his Maxims of Parsimony and went away in a Stage-Coach; nor did his Friends expect to hear from him till he informed them of his Arrival in Swansea.

But when they least expected, arrived a Letter dated the fourteenth Day after his Departure, in which he sent them Word, that he was yet upon the Road, and without Money; and he therefore could not proceed without a Remittance. They sent him the Money that was in their hands, with which he was able to reach Bristol from whence he was to go to Swansea by water.

After some stay in Bristol he retired to Swansea, the Place originally proposed for his residence, where he lived for about a Year, very much dissatisfied with the Diminution of his Salary; but contracted, as in other Places, Acquaintances with those who were most distinguished in that Country, among whom he has celebrated Mr Powel and Mrs Jones, by some Verses which he inserted in the Gentleman's Magazine.

EPITAPH ON MRS JONES, GRANDMOTHER TO MRS BRIDGET JONES OF LLANELLY, CARMARTHENSHIRE

In her, whose relics mark this sacred earth,
Shone all domestic and all social worth:
First, Heav'n her hope with early offspring crown'd;
And then a second race rose numerous round.
Heav'n to industrious virtue blessing lent.
And all was competence, and all content.
Though frugal care, in Wisdom's eye admired,
Knew to preserve what industry acquired;
Yet, at her board, with decent plenty blest,
The journeying stranger sat a welcome guest.
Prest on all sides, did trading neighbours fear
Ruin, which hung o'er exigence severe?
Farewell the friend, who spar'd the assistant loan —
A neighbour's woe or welfare was her own.
Did piteous lazars oft attend her door?
She gave — farewell, the parent of the poor:
Youth, age and want, once cheer'd, now sighing swell,
Bless her loved name, and weep a last farewell.

In Swansea Savage completed his Tragedy, of which two Acts were wanting when he left London; and was desirous of coming to Town, to bring it upon the Stage. This Design was warmly opposed; and he was advised, by his chief Benefactor, to put it in the hands of Mr Thomson and Mr Mallett. This Proposal he rejected with the utmost Contempt. He attemped to promote a Subscription for his Works, and formed a Resolution of leaving this Part of the Country, to which he thought it not reasonable to be confined, and, with an intent to return to London, went to Bristol. He was soon in Prison for Debt.

His Time for the most Part was spent in Study, or in receiving Visits: but sometimes he descended to lower Amusements, and diverted himself in the Kitchen with the Conversation of Criminals. The last Time the Keeper saw him was on July 31st, when Savage, seeing him at his bedside, said, with an uncommon Earnestness, 'I have something to say to you, Sir,' but after a pause moved his Hand in a melancholy Manner: unable to recollect what he was going to communicate said, 'Tis gone!' The Keeper soon left him; and the next morning he died.

Such were the life and death of Richard Savage, a man, equally distinguished by his Virtues and Vices; and at once remarkable for his Weaknesses and Abilities.

15. Boswell, James. Life of Johnson. Ed: G. B. Hill, Clarendon Press, pp. 161-174.

16. Johnson, Samuel. Life of Richard Savage, F. Newbery, 1775. pp. 141, 163, 165.

17. Works of Richard Savage. Stanhope Press. 1807. p. 176.

James Boswell. 1740-1795.

Samuel Johnson. 1709-1784.

'The most remarkable person Johnson consorted with c.1738, was Richard Savage, an earl's son, a shoemaker's apprentice, who had seen life in all its forms. He had sunk into abject and hopeless poverty. His pen had failed him and his patrons had died or become estranged by his extravagance and insolence. He lived by begging. Yet in his misery he was an agreeable companion. During some months he lived in closest familiarity with Johnson. Soon after the death of Savage, while public curiosity was strongly excited about his extraordinary adventures, a life appeared widely different from the catchpenny lives of eminent men. The style was indeed deficient in ease and variety; and the writer too partial to the Latin element of our language. But the little work, with all its faults, was a masterpiece. No finer specimen of literary biography existed in any language, living or dead. The Life of

Savage was anonymous; but it was well known in literary circles that Johnson was the writer.'

Enc. Brit.

Richard Savage. c. 1697-1743
Supposed illegitimate son of Lady Macclesfield and Richard Savage, 4th earl of Rivers.
Born at Fox Court; boarded out in Jan 1697 and afterwards unrecorded; denounced as an impostor by Lady Macclesfield, then Brett, in 1718.
In Swansea he lived in Barber Court, near the pre-war site of Capel Gomer, now the Kingsway Roundabout.

A SURGEON'S MATE FROM GLAMORGAN

In this garb, Captain Whiffle, for that was his name, took possession of the ship, surrounded by a crowd of attendants, all of whom, in their different degrees, seemed to be of their patron's disposition; and the air was so impregnated with perfumes, that one may venture to affirm the clime of Arabia Felix was not half so sweet scented. My fellow-mate, observing no surgeon among his train, thought he had found an occasion too favourable for himself to be neglected; and remembering the old proverb, 'Spare to speak, and spare to speed!' resolved to solicit the new captain's interest immediately, before any other surgeon could be appointed for the ship. With this view he repaired to the cabin in ordinary dress, consisting of a check shirt and trousers, a brown linen waistcoat, and a nightcap of the same (neither of them very clean), which for his future misfortune, happened to smell strong of tobacco. Entering without any ceremony into this sacred place, he found Captain Whiffle reposing on a couch, with a wrapper of fine chintz about his body, and a muslin cap bordered with lace about his head; and after several low congees, began in this manner: 'Sir, I hope you will forgive, and excuse and pardon the presumption of one who has not the honour of being known unto you, but who is, nevertheless, a shentleman porn and pred, and moreover has had misfortunes, Got help me in the world.'

Here he was interrupted by the Captain, who, on seeing him, had started up with great amazement at the novelty of the apparition and having recollected himself, pronounced, with a look and tone signifying disdain, curiosity, and surprise. 'Zauns, who art thou?'

'I am a surgeon's first mate on board of this ship,' replied Morgan, 'and I most vehemently desire and beseech you, with all submission to be pleased to condescend, and vouchsafe to inquire into my character, and my pehaviour, and my deserts, which under Got, I hope will entitle me to the vacancy of surgeon.'

As he proceeded in his speech, he continued advancing toward the captain, whose nostrils were no sooner saluted with the aromatic flavour that exhaled from him than he cried with great emotion, 'Heaven preserve me! I am suffocated. Fellow, fellow, away with thee. Curse the fellow! get thee gone, I shall be stunk to death!'

At the noise of his outcries his servants ran into his apartment, and he accosted them thus, 'Villains! Cut-throats! Traitors! I am betrayed. I am sacrificed! Will you not carry that monster away? Or must I be stifled with the stench of him. Oh! Oh!'

His valet de chambre plied him with a smelling bottle: one footman chafed his temples with Hungary water; another sprinkled the floor with spirits of lavender; a third pushed Morgan out of the cabin, who coming to the place where I was, sat down with a demure countenance; and according to his custom, when he received any indignity which he durst not revenge began to sing a Welsh ditty. I guessed he was under sore agitation of spirits, and desired to know the cause; but, instead of answering me directly, he asked, with great emotion, if I thought him a monster and a stinkard.

'A monster and a stinkard!' said I, with some surprise; 'did anybody call you so?'

'Got is my judge,' replied he, 'Captain Fifle did call me both, aye, and all the water of the Tawe will not wash it out of my remembrance. I do affirm, and avouch, and maintain, with all my soul and pody, and my plood, look you, that I have not smells about me but such as a Christian ought to have, except the effluvia of tobacco, which is a cephalic, odiferous, aromatick herb, and he is the son of a mountain goat who says otherwise. As for my being a monster, let that be as it is. I am as Got pleased to create me, which peradventure, is more than I shall aver of him that gave me the title; for I will proclaim it before the world, that he is disguised, and transfigured, and transmogrified, with affectation, and whimsies; and that he is more like a papoon than one of the human race!'

18. Smollett, Tobias. The Adventure of Roderick Random. Hanson and Co., London. 1790. Vol. I. pp. 122-3.

Tobias Smollett 1721-1771

Left Scotland in 1739.
Described journey in Roderick Random. 1748.
Surgeon's mate on H.M.S. Cumberland.
Scott claimed that every writer on the navy since seems to have copied more from Smollett than from nature.

Enc. Brit.

SWANSEA SEA CHANTY

1. Oh farewell to you my Nancy, ten thousand times adieu;
I'm bound to cross the ocean girl, once more to part from you.
Once more to part from you, fine girl, you're the girl that I adore
But still I live in hopes to see old Swansea town once more.

Old Swansea town once more, my girl, you're the girl that I adore
But still I live in hopes to see old Swansea town once more.

2. Oh, it's now that I am out to sea, and you are far behind;
Kind letters I will write to you of the secrets of my mind
The secrets of my mind, fine girl, you're the girl that I adore
But still I live in hopes to see old Swansea town once more.

3. Oh now the storm it's rising, I can see it coming on
The night so dark as anything, we cannot see the moon
Our good old ship she is toss'd aft, our rigging is all tore
But still I live in hopes to see old Swansea town once more.

4. Oh now the storm is over and we are safe on shore
We'll drink strong drinks and brandies too, to the girls that we adore

To the girls that we adore, fine girls, we'll make this tavern roar
And when our money is all gone we'll go to sea for more.

Old Swansea town etc.

Folksong—Collected by G. B. Gardiner. Music by G. Holst Curwen 61088, 1917.

THE MORRIS FAMILY

Robert Morris d 1768	m 1725	Margaret Jenkins d 1786

Robert 1743-93 barrister	John 1745-1819 knighted 1806	4 surviving daughters

NOTE. Robert Morris of Cleobury and Bishop's Castle married Margaret Jenkins of Machynlleth at St. John's Church (now St. Matthew's) on Sept. 5, 1725. In 1727, with others he took over the Llangyfelach Copper Works at Landore. He bought the estates of Tredegar Fawr and Penderi Fawr, Llangyfelach, and Ynysarwel, Neath. He also had a house in Swansea. He died at his London home in Mortimer Street in 1768. He is buried at St. John's Church with his wife, 'four of his dear deceased children,' his son, Sir John Morris, and his wife, formerly Lady Henrietta Musgrave.

'I may truly say of my dear father, upon the most mature and cool reflection, that no one ever saw him without respecting him — His amiable manner, his Countenance, his deportment, Language and voice, in fact every word and every action announced the good man, as well as the accomplished Englishman of his day — He never spoke with anger nor ruled with austerity; and there was in him and irresistible and undescribable something which at the same time both commanded your respect and increased your love. Was I to speak of his unaffected piety and his unbounded affection for his children and of his good will to all men, it would seem to exceed all necessary and reasonable limits.'

19. Morris, Sir John. Unpublished noetbook. U.C.S. Lib.

WILL OF ROBERT MORRIS (June 1768)

Whenever the Almighty God in whose pleasure the hours of life and death are, puts a period to my Existaunce in this world all the Estate and substance he has or may be pleased to favour me with I give, devise and bequeath by this my will and Testament as followeth.

First I give to my Dear beloved wife Margaret Morris the use and occupying of my dwelling house in Swansea, if she chuses to consider it together with the use of all my furniture and plate my chaise and chaise horses for and during the term she surives me. I likewise give to my said beloved wife all my estate in Lands called Tredegar in the parish of Llangwevelach together with all the stock of cattle corn Implements of husbandry and household furniture there at the time of my decease for and during the term of her life likewise my estate called Masmillan in the said parish of Llanguvelach for her life and the profit of the Green Hill Mill which I hold by lease from the Duke of Beaufort. Also the lands of Inheritance called Cadwgan Penllan Owen and Gwair Tire' in the County of Montgomery and also the sum of six hundred pounds

secondly I give to my daughter Margaret Morris the sum of fifteen hundred pounds besides the one fourth part of my share and interest in the capital stock of the Rope Trade, now carrying on in Swansea together with the profits accruing thereby in like manner as I have for some time past allowed her to receive it

thirdly I give to my daughter Mary Morris the sum of fifteen hundred pounds besides the one fourth part of my share and interest in the capital stock of the Rope trade in Swansea with the profits accruing thereby in the manner as I have for time past allowed her to receive and enjoy the same

fourthly I give to my daughter Jane Morris the sum of fifteen hundred pounds besides the one fourth part of my share and interest in the Swansea Rope Trade with the profits accruing thereby in like manner as I have hitherto allowed her to receive it

fifthly I give to my daughter Bridget wife of Thomas Lockwood Esquire the other one fourth of my share and interest in the Swansea Rope Trade together with the profits accruing thereby as I have hitherto given her the same annually and I give to my two grand-daughters Bridget Lockwood and Matilda Lockwood two hundred pounds to be paid them by my executors hereinafter named when they respectively attain the age of eighteen

sixth I give and bequeath to my son Robert Morris now of Lincoln's Inn esquire the reversion of all my lands and tenements before mentioned after the decease of his mother and from the time of my decease I give him my estate called Pengravenny in the parish of Llanrhidian in the County of Glamorgan My estate called Pwlar Oir in the parish of Llanguvelach and my house in the strand wherein Thomas Lott dwells Likewise three of my shares in the capital stock of the Copper Trade and collierys in which I am a copartner with John Lockwood Esquire and others and I also give to my said son the sum of five hundred pounds

seventh I give to my son John Morris my estate of Penrhiwallin with its appurtenances in the manor of Clase in the parish of Llanguvelach I also give to him two shares in the capital stock of the copper trade coalerys in which I am copartner with John Lockwood Esquire and others and whereas by the articles of Copartnership in the business — the shares on trust now belonging to Mrs. Hester Gibbon are on the event of her marriage or death to become the property of Mr. John Lockwood and myself at the rate or value they shall then stand in at the last annual balance of the company's books — my will and desire is that my son John Morris should at that event take my right of preemption to a moiety of Mrs Gibbons shares according to the articles of the copartnership I also give to my said son John my moiety of the stock cattle horses hay corn goods and implements with all profit in the farm of Lower Forest in which I am jointly interested with my brother Thomas Morris and I give to my said son John the sum of two hundred ponds

I give my sister Jane Morris the sum of fifty pounds I give to my brother Thomas Morris the sum of fifty pounds I give to my servant Thomas Lott the sum of ten pounds Lastly I constitute and appoint my sons Robert and John Morris joint Executors of this my will and testament and to be my residuary legatees after their paying all my debts and legacies

If I die in or near Swansea let me be buried in the Church of St. John where I buried four of my dear deceased children and

to the mercy of my Gracious God I commend my soul
This is my last will and testament written with my own hand and sealed with my seal this twentyfirst day of February in the Year of our Lord one thousand seven hundred and sixty eight.
28th May 1768 Robert Morris duly sworn Power reserved to John Morris.

20. Ref: Secker 248 Somerset House.

THE BARONETCY OF SIR JOHN MORRIS OF CLASEMONT

Cause of my baronetcy.
Lord Bute wrote as follows when Mr Addington was Minister to J.M.

I recommend you to obtain an audience of the Minister and there state your pretensions. They are as follows, upon the County of Glamorgan coming so handsomely forward in raising volunteers it was suggested and agreed to by the Government in the person of Mr Dundas bestow upon some one gentleman the Dignity of Baronet and you were accordingly pointed out.

This is the true and exact state of the business.

I remain,
Yours most sincerely,
Bute.

The Baronetcy was promised to Lord Bute by Mr Pitt during his domin^{n} but did not take place. Ld. B. being hostile to Mr A., nothing was done till Mr Fox came in when it was among the first acts of the kind.

21. Morris, Sir John. Unpublished notebook. U.C.S. Lib.

THE BUILDING OF ST. JOHN'S CHURCH, MORRISTON

To the Earl of Liverpool. Clasemont July 8, 1817

My Lord,

My very esteemed friend Mr Hall inform'd me, how much I ow'd to your Lordship's favourable intention to promote my son,

The Rev'd Thomas Morris to some preferment in the Church, whenever he might be able to point out precisely what might be vacant in your Lordship's Gift, or in the Lord Chancellor's and on the 26th of June he wrote to me from Brighton (just as I left Mr Legge's at Putney) that understanding the Living of Allhallow's London Wall was vacant and in the gift of the Lord Chancellor that he shou'd by the following Post address a Letter to your Lordship on the occasion, as he felt himself quite unequal to writing that day, Since that I am sorry to say he has been attacked by a violent inflammation of the lungs, that has prevented from putting his intention in execution, which I am certain he will do, the first moment his health permits him.

Under the circumstances, and least the Lord Chancellor might in the interval bestow the Living of Allhallows on some other Clergyman, I trust your Lordship's goodness will pardon me, as a Father, for thus intruding myself, and that I may be permitted, to give a short and faithful description of my son's eligibility to fill the sought for preferment.

After having been educated at Eton, he removed to Oriel College, Oxford, of which University he is now a Member, where he pass'd as I was inform'd an examination much to his credit, both for his Bachelor and Masters Degree; He has been ten years in Orders without any Church preferment, tho' the Duke of Beaufort has warmly solicited the Lord Chancellor to promote him to a stall, either at Gloucester or Bristol, and he has not been without a zealous friend in the present Lord Chief Baron, at present however he remains the Curate of Kingston on Thames where I have had the gratification to hear, he has done the duty of that extensive Parish, much to the satisfaction of the Parishioners.

Will your Lordship also permit me to add one other plea, tho' it might savour somewhat of vanity on my part, It is this, that living in a very large Parish, where the Mother Church was above eight miles from parts of it, many, very many indeed, had become dissenters from the establish'd Religion. I was induced, several years ago, to build and endow a Chapel of Ease at my own expense, and for which I have repeatedly receiv'd the thanks of the several Bishops of St David's who have succeeded to that See.

I have the honour to remain with all due respect

Your Lordship's, most obliged and faithful

Hum. Servt

John Morris

NOTE. The letter has the following note by the Earl of Liverpool.

Ans'd to the same effect as the answer to Mr Hall's application in favor of Mr Morris.

22. Add. MSS. 38267 f.289 B.M. Lib.

APOLOGY TO THE EARL OF LIVERPOOL BY SIR JOHN

My Lord,

I must entreat your Lordship's pardon for the liberty I take, in acknowledging the honor you have done me, in replying to my letter of the 8th. but without doing so, I feel it possible that I may have been misunderstood by your Lordship in stating what I had done, under an idea, that your reply to Mr Hall might have been known to me at the time.

My friend Mr. Hall did certainly give me reason to understand that your Lordship, had not only reply'd most favourably to his request on the part of my Son, as to the preferment in your Lordship's gift, but as he understood it, also if anything suitable occurr'd in the gift of the Lord Chancellor.

However to the latter, he seems to have been under a mistake, Therefore if the Case I might endeavour to make out on the part of my Son, did not come within the exceptions wh. your Lordship has detailed, I can only return my grateful thanks, for the assurance you were so good as to make, that whenever any Church preferment, within the gift of your Lordship was pointed out, an application on the part of my Son, wou'd be favourably received.

I have the honour to remain with all due respect

Your L's most obliged and faithful Hum[l] S[t]

J. Morris.

Clasemont, 13th July 1817

22. Add MSS. 38267 f.289. B.M. Lib.

THE BUILDING OF MORRIS TOWN c.1779

Clasemont.

Feb. 25 1819

To the Earl of Liverpool.

My Lord,

Nothing but a belief that I might possibly throw some light upon a question of great magnitude cou'd have induced me to have taken the liberty of intruding myself upon your Lordship, which I respectfully trust you will have the goodness to excuse, and I feel rather the more competent to do so, from having resided during a long life in the County of Glamorgan, a County wh. from its comparative size, will I apprehend be found to contain a much greater mass of coal, than any other in the Kingdom, wh. had led to the establishment of various manufactorys within these forty years, hardly to be credited.

In the Village of Merthyr Tidvil, wh. I recollect only to have contain'd half a dozen thatch'd Cottages, now possesses a population of more than 12000, where the iron trade is carried on, to a wonderful extent.

The Town of Swansea, wh. I recollect had not 2000 inhabitants, has now more than 6 times that no; In this neighbourhood, much the greatest quantity of Copper Ore is smelted, that is rais'd in the kingdom, probably not less than Forty thou: tons p.ann. tho' ninety years ago it can be proved by undoubted documents, that the whole quantity of Copper Ore raised annually in the Co. of Cornwall did not exceed 10,000 tons. I will not trouble your Lordship, (in detail) on the rapid improvements in Agriculture, which have taken place within these last fifty years, all arising as

I could clearly prove, from the facility with wh. Coal is obtained, unfettered with a tax.

At present the poor rates wh. bear so heavy on the Farmer are kept down in a degree, from the various classes having in great measure, their fuel gratis, which with a potatoe ground annex'd to their Cottages, enables them when industrious to bring up their family in a decent manner.

About 40 years ago I appropriated a farm for the purpose of inducing the artificers and labourers of the County, to build thereon giving them a long term of years, at a nominal acknowlegement with a sufficient plot laid on, for raising Potatoes. The scheme at the time was thought a visionary one, by all around me; but I have lived to see, about 300 stone cottages, with tiled Roofs, built by this class of persons, & I need not add that such persons never become burthensome to their Parish but continue to hold out the best example of prudence to their neighbours.

Upon a first view of the subject, the inequality of the Coal duties, may strike some persons as partial & unjust, but an enlightened mind need not be, furnish'd with many arguments wh. occur to prove the contrary, & there is one simple fact wh. I beg to notice to your Lordship, that if the duties were to be made equal, the quality of the Coal, to be tax'd, shou'd also be equal; whereas it can be proved that a great proportion of the Coal, capable of being work'd in this County, is not two thirds of the value of Newcastle Coal, & finds only its consumption in consequence of its cheapness —

I can assure your Lordship, to make it a practicable tax, I believe to be hardly possible, but of this I am certain, that 'till something is settled, respecting that momentous evil, the Laws respecting the Poor, the proposed tax on coal had better be postponed. Considering how locally connected I am with the subject, my judgement, may I feel be considered as unduly biassed — as far as I am able to search myself, it is not so, & as a proof of it, I do think the most beneficial effects, to the state wou'd arise from an abolition of all Coal duties whatever, from wh. advantages wou'd arise in my humble opinion beyond all present calculation, & if an equivalent p/centage was added to some of the existing taxes, an answer wou'd at once be given to what is now unfairly considered, as unjust advantage to the coal county's.

I have the honor to remain with great respect

Your Lordship's most obliged & obed. Humb[l]

Serv[t] John Morris.

22. Add. MSS. 38275 f.1332. B.M. Lib.

THE DESTRUCTION OF THE TAWE VALLEY

We pursued it (the river) no further, but, after visiting the remains of Neath Abbey, crossed a hill to reach those numerous collieries and copper-works, which occupying an immense tract of country towards Swansea, blast the soil all around with their sulphureous influence, destroying the appearance of verdure, and preventing cultivation. These works formed by several spirited proprietors, are chiefly conducted by Mr. Morris, whose handsome seat of Clasemont overlooks the whole territory: all the hills around are covered with their buildings, and the principal assemblage of houses, formed into regular streets with a church and wharfs, bears the title Morris-town. Through this curious place, and amidst all that train of villas and abundant population which indicate the prosperity arising from successful enterprise we approached the walls of Swansea, now swelled into a port of great importance, from its neighbouring manufactures.

23. Skrine, Henry. Two Successive tours throughout the whole of Wales. Emsley and Bremner. 1798. p. 8.

ROBERT MORRIS AND THE FIGHT FOR THE FREEDOM OF THE PRESS AND LIBERTY OF THE SUBJECT

ROBERT MORRIS 1743-1793
Baptised at St. Mary's Swansea.
Oriel College Oxford. 1760-1764
Called to the Bar 1767
Joined the Society of the Supporters of the Bill of Rights.

Elected first secretary Feb. 20, 1769.
Involved in quarrel between John Wilkes and the Rev. Horne Took.

Resigned as secretary September 1770.
Eloped with his ward, May 1772.
Marriages abroad declared illegal and annulled in 1784.
Married Sarah Prichard of Bach y Gwreiddyn, Llangyfelach in 1785.

Died in India in 1793.

JOHN WILKES. 1727-97

Elected M.P. in 1757; active opponent of Lord Bute.
Founded the North Briton in 1762; arrested for libel in 1763.
Expelled from Westminster; abroad for 4 years, returning secretly for short periods.
Re-elected to Parliament in 1769 but expelled for another libel and imprisoned.
Elected 3 times for Middlesex but not allowed to sit until 1790.
Lord Mayor in 1774.
City Chamberlain 1779-97.
Supported American colonists against England.

Letter from Mr. Robert Morris to John Wilkes, May 27, 1770.
Lincoln's Inn

Sir,

I am unwilling to interfere in the dispute between you and Mr Horne who have both deserved well of the public, and are so fully qualified to fight your own battles but as I perceive a mistake in your last letter, where you mention my name, which it is in my power to correct, and as it is a position agreed, that people have a right to the truth, I cannot by my silence admit you to have given an exact representation of your conduct respecting Mr. Horne's letter from Montpellier.

The sentiment you would have the world adopt is that the first reproduction of that letter was in consequence of what I said, and to corroborate your answer: Therefore not a wanton or designed publication of a private and confidential letter. I am persuaded that no conversation passed between us wh. can justify such a conclusion upon your conduct.

I first heard of the letter, not from yourself but from persons to whom you had previously shown it and it was 1st produced to me at the Devil Tavern called the Retribution Club where I believe I was at that time the only stranger to its contents amidst a dozen other gentlemen in the room, and before which time you had never spoken to me of such a letter.

As to the parties who are contesting, I have no reason to wish success on one side more than on another; and I shall certainly not decide upon such a dispute till it is ended. As yet I may say with Lucan, Quis justius induit arma scire nefas; magno se iudice quisque tuetur.

It is the cause of liberty I wish to promote and I care not by whose hand it triumphs. Of that cause alone I desire to be esteemed a partisan, and not of any individual.

Robert Morris.

NOTE. In his reply Wilkes denied Robert Morris's assertion and challenged him to prove he had not previously discussed Horne, and declared that the letter was produced specifically to support what Morris had discussed with him. After the July meeting of the Supporters of the Bill of Rights many of the most respectable members talked of quitting the Society over Wilkes' debts.

24. Controversial Letters of John Wilkes and Rev. Horne. Williams, 1771 pp. 107-9

THE QUARREL BETWEEN THE REVEREND HORNE AND JOHN WILKES OVER ROBERT MORRIS'S LETTER OF THANKS TO SOUTH CAROLINA

NOTE. The Bill of rights Society in South Carolina sent a donation to Britain in support of Wilkes's cause in February, 1770. Horne accused Wilkes of hating America and of wanting to send a letter of thanks drawn up by Robert Morris which was indiscreet.

Princes Court. June 14, 1770

Mr. Morris, the secretary at the time, drew up an answer, which he shewed to me, first in the rough draft, and afterwards finished.

It was diffuse, but sensible and spirited. I approved it but did not commend it warmly to any of my friends, for it contained many compliments to me personally. On this account I know that you disliked it. You complained that Mr. Morris was a mad man, that the letter was execrable, and would bring the Society disgrace. I said that perhaps the letter might be thought here rather too diffuse and copious, but Mr Morris had considered it was proper to give the g/men of S. Carolina a full exposition of the sentiments of the Society: that in America our brethren were more studious of expressing themselves with force and clearness than with conciseness and classical energy: that the copious style was theirs: that their own productions abounded more in reasoning than elegance of diction: that they often preferred to our close style a diffuse mode of writing, to avoid possibility of any doubt of their meaning: that in this style Mr Morris excelled: that I should even regret their rivalling Europe in the meretricious arts of eloquence, fine writing and polite literature, for they wd probably make such acquisitions at the expence of strength of thought and manliness of sentiment, in wh. they excelled the Europeans: that we ourselves were greatly deficient: that most of the modern refinements of Europe were the luxurious effects of a debauched vitiated, enervated taste, wh. had lost sight of the antient and true elegance of simplicity: that very few among the Americans had in fact succeeded in either of the sister arts of poetry or painting: that spirit, not taste, was their characters: that I knew no fault in Mr. Morris's letter, except the compliments to myself: that language was, after all, merely the dress of our thoughts: and that it was peevish and ill-bred to find fault with Mr Morris, only because periods of strong sense were not tuned to the nice ear of Mr Horne. These were the sentiments I expressed to you, and many of my friends. I was never with the committee. The transaction happened during my imprisonment. At the London Tavern I am told that you were furious and unmannerly about the secretary's letter. Mr. Morris in a good-natured manner, withdrew his intended answer to the gentlemen of S. Carolina. You produced another letter wh. was at length adopted. I desire an explanation of what you mean by extraordinary measures I have given the whole of this business. Will you prevail on your new friend Mr. Morris to favour the public with his intended answer; and will you give us your own uncastrated letter as it was first proposed to the Bill of Rights.

24. Controversial Letters. p. 167.

Horne is described as 'a robust little dandy with only one eye, flaunting thro' the Continent in very unclerical suits of flowered silk and gold lace, the son of a rich man in his care.'

LETTER OF RESIGNATION

Sept. 4 1770

Mr Morris late secretary to the Society of the Supporters of the Bill of Rights has declined that office and accordingly written a letter to the chairman which concludes with the following paragraph:

For my own part I will confess, that the cause of Mr Wilkes, as an injured and persecuted individual, has been the first and hitherto the only motive of my appearing in public. I have the satisfaction to say, that I leave this cause in a better situation, at least than when I found it; though not the vanity to think, that much of our success (wh. indeed ought to have been greater) has been owing to my endeavours. I am resolved however not to act any longer in the office of secretary. I should not have undertaken it at first, but in expectation that it would soon have fallen to the lot of others in turn. I have repeatedly desired to resign, and as constantly received no other answer than your compliments to my conduct. I must now therefore resign without leave, because I cannot continue in my office with the same alacrity I have done, being tired of my share of the burden, and having something else to do. As for the odium wh. may have fallen on my name, from the conspicuous part I have appeared in, I shall esteem that my greatest reward, being satisfied it will only come from a quarter, whose enmity will be my greatest honour. When you proceed to the election of another secretary I hope your choice will fall on one more worthy than

Gentlemen etc. etc.

Robert Morris.

25. Town and Country Magazine. 1770 p. 500

ROBERT MORRIS'S INVITATION TO WILKES

Oct. 9. 1770

I conceive by this time most of your great City business wch seem'd to detain you in town, is concluded, and, what is more, happily so. You have therefore nothing to do now, but to take a ramble with your friend in this part of Wales. I know many good houses where you wd have as good a welcome, but it is the Country and the open air, that I imagine wd suit your taste the best. If Mountain, Rivers, Seas can charm, here you may have your fill; in short we have all sorts of prospects I think, and all sorts of animals to command, but women, for whom I shall say nothing. I don't know indeed, what conquests you may be able to make, for you are certainly a great favourite with the Ladies. There is one, a very elegant creature & former acquaintance of yours Mrs Gomm, who dies to see you; & will have this advantage besides, that she has retired into the Country having parted from her husband. I write this from Hanbury's at Pontipool, & am now going with a large Glamorganshire party to the Races at Monmouth; from thence I return to Cowbridge in Glamorganshire, whither if you form an early resolution, & write to me by return of the Post, I shd be most happy to meet an appointment from you to come & conduct you from Bath, Bristol or the Passage upon whatever Schemes & to whatever part of the Country you please. At least let me have the pleasure of learning some of your intentions by as early a letter, as you can write, and I remain, with much esteem.

yr sincere friend,

R. Morris.

26. Add. MSS. 30871. f.40 B.M. Lib.

Wilkes had been released from prison in April, 1770 — he did not accept the invitation. Pontypool Park was the home of John Hanbury, M.P. for Monmouthshire.

ROBERT MORRIS'S ARGUMENT FOR THE RELEASE OF PRINTERS ARRESTED FOR PUBLISHING PRESS REPORTS

Mr. Chairman,

The proclamation issued for apprehending the printers is on all hands, I think, allowed to be illegal. I do not believe that there is in the whole kingdom a lawyer's clerk who does not know it to be equally repugnant to the spirit and letter of the law and the constitution. The law, though not so well known is as clear against commitments by the house of Commons. They have nothing to support their pretensions but their own vote, wh. certainly is not binding on any but themselves; an act of the 3 branches of the legislature being the only authority that is, besides the common law, acknowledged by England as valid. Matters being thus circumstanced, I am sorry to find that such magistrates of London, as belong to this Society, do not afford protection to the printers and rescue them from lawless violence.

My concern for this neglect, this fear, or this tergiversation, is the greater, that, if the officers of the house of Commons, or any other person but a minister of the city properly authorized, takes these obnoxious men into custody the rights of the city are violated; it being legally impossible for King, Lords and Commons to seize any citizen of London without consent of its own magistrates. Were they even to make an act for that purpose, it could not have any force; because the act made in favour of the city, in the reign of William and Mary, ought to be considered as a constitution and as irreversible as Magna Carta; for indeed it is the Magna Carta of the city. For all these reasons, it gives me pain to see the printers deserted; and I wish Mr Alderman Townsend were present, that I might complain to him face to face, of his having forfeited his word by refusing to be the man who would release them if they were apprehended in consequence of this illegal proclamation. Indeed I have already talked to him on the subject & asked why he did not perform his promise? His answer was that he did not find he should be supported by any great man, and otherwise it would be folly.

27. Controversial Letters of John Wilkes. Williams.
Note. The speech was made at the Meeting of the Supporters of the Bill of Rights, March, 12, 1771, that is, after Morris's resignation as secretary.

LETTER BY JUNIUS

I have two observations to make upon the late attempt of

enforcing the order of the House of Commons by the royal proclamation.

First, that the calling in the aid of the King upon that occasion was weakening the authority and dignity of the House, and tends to make the execution of the orders of that House dependent upon the pleasure of the King; and in the next place such an interposition on the part of the King carries this appearance with it to the public, that it is not the independence or the just liberties and privileges of the Commons of England that are anxiously sought to be preserved, but the gratification of the spleen and resentment (to say no worse of it) of the administration.

I shall conclude this letter by saying, and thinking till I am better informed, that the late proclamation was an unwarrantable exertion of power, tending to mislead all judges and justices throughout England, and to put them upon imprisoning an English subject contrary to law and the rules of evidence, wh. make part of the law of this kingdom; and therefore I, for one, applaud the conduct of Mr Wilkes in this instance.

In another letter I shall deliver my sentiments as to the proceedings of your Lordship, Mr Alderman Oliver and Mr. Alderman Wilkes, when the messenger of the House of Commons was brought before you. I have forborne to take this business up on the same grounds as Mr Morris has done, as it would only be a repetition of what he has very judiciously before transmitted to the public. It is sufficient for me to say that I think he has sufficiently demonstrated the illegality of the order of the House of Commons: I only meant to give additional strength to his observations.

I am, My Lord & Gmen,

Your most humble servant, G.W.

March 29, 1771.

28. Wade, John. Junius. H. G. Bohn, London. 1850. Vol. 2. p. 355

WILLIAM HICKEY ON ROBERT MORRIS

Robert Morris had made himself particularly conspicuous as a violent patriot in the days of Wilkes' popularity, of whose cause he was for some time an enthusiastic supporter. Upon the establishment of the Society formed in order to relieve and uphold their idol (Wilkes) calling themselves the 'Bill of Rights,' in the year 1768, or somewhere about that period, Mr Morris was peculiarly active, voluntarily offering to officiate in the troublesome situation of Secretary.

His proffered services being thankfully accepted, he was in consequence, when alluded to in any of the public prints, distinguished by the title of 'Bill of Rights' Morris.

After acting for a considerable time with much apparent zeal, his ardour ceased, and he tendered his resignation of the Secretaryship, at which members in general were greatly surprized, some of whom took the liberty of asking his reason for wishing to secede, a question he bluffly replied to by saying, 'He had something else to do.' From which circumstance the waggish writers for the newspapers changed his title, and he was thenceforward designated as 'Something else to do Morris.' which title he retained until the time of his running away with Miss Harford, an heiress, whom he married, and then conveyed to the Continent.

While this business with the lady was under discussion in the newspapers, he underwent a third change of title, being then described as 'The Harford heiress Morris.'

Finally the marriage was pronounced null and void. As to her person he was disposed to relinquish that without compunction, being as tired of her as she could possibly be of him, but with respect to the fortune it was quite another thing. That had become indispensibly necessary to enable him to continue living in the style he had adopted, upon his connexion with her. He therefore fought his way inch by inch, but ultimately was obliged to yield.

In the month of December, 1791, Morris arrived in Calcutta with an intention of practising as an Advocate.

A few days after his arrival, which happened to be in Term time, he addressed a letter to each of the four Judges, wherein he informed them of the date of his being called to the Bar of the Court of King's Bench at Westminster, and that his object in coming to Bengal was to practise as an Advocate in the Supreme Court.

An answer was sent to Mr Morris that the Judges did not consider it either prudent or just to increase their number. Sir

William Dunkin proposed sending the rejection in direct terms without evasion, by assigning the actual reason for their refusing his demand, but the other Judges conceived such a proceeding might be unnecessarily wounding the feelings of a man who perhaps had seen his errors and resolved upon a complete reformation.

Upon receipt of the answer through the principal officer of the Court, Mr Morris again addressed the Judges, and told them that he never meant to ask, nor did he expect or wish for the smallest favour from their hands, either jointly or individually; as a Barrister of the highest Court in England he contended he had a right to plead in any inferior Court he might choose to enter: that he should therefore attend in the Supreme Court of Calcutta the following morning.

No notice whatever being taken of this second address, Morris made his appearance the next day equipped in gown, band, and wig, and upon the Judges taking their seats upon the Bench he rose, and in an eloquent speech renewed his claim of being permitted to plead as an Advocate.

The Chief Justice said he did not consider himself bound to give any other reason than he had already done. Morris then interrupted the Judge violently exclaiming, 'Then I will make you individually and personally responsible for your illegal and wanton tyranny.'

Mr Justice Hyde, offended at his conduct, said, 'You had better be more circumspect and guarded in your expressions.'

Sir William Dunkin next addressed him, 'Mr. Robert Morris, you have in very unbecoming and indecorous language called upon the Judges to assign their specific reasons for refusing to allow of your practicing as an Advocate. I have no hesitation in publishing to the whole world what my sentiments are upon the occasion. I object to your being admitted an Advocate of the Court from the notoriety and infamy of your character, and from the vile, abandoned, and disgraceful life you have led for many years past.' Morris appeared to be utterly confounded; after shewing the utmost agitation, he suddenly left the Court without uttering another syllable.

Shortly after this Morris went up the country, making himself conspicuous by his violent conduct wherever he remained twelve hours.

Happily for society this dangerous and troublesome man was carried off by an attack of liver about eight months after he left Calcutta.

29. Hickey, William. Memoirs. 1791-2. Adapted from Ch. V.

FROM JOHN MORRIS'S NOTEBOOK

Nov. 29th, 1793. This day my poor brother was buried at Futtygharh, in the East Indies.
Probably the Fategharh now in Uttar Pradesh. See I.O.R. N/1/4/153.

'Attach yourselves to those most nearly allied to you for the ties of blood are most to be depended on.

30. Morris, John: Notebook. U.C.S. Lib.

NOTE. Hickey's account is incorrect in several details.
The Bill of Rights Society met in 1769.
Morris went through two marriage ceremonies abroad.
He did not return with Miss Harford to England nor keep her a close prisoner.
His diary records his deep distress on her leaving him in Paris in 1774.
He was condemned to the Fleet Prison for contmept of Court in failing to produce Miss Harford on Aug. 5. 1772.
In June 1782 he was excommunicated for failing to appear at the Court of Delegates: in October he was "produced for his answer to the Libel brought against him."

Assignation Book. P.R. Office.

THE NEED FOR A BRIDGE

The approach to the town would be rendered much more agreeable and convenient, as well to the inhabitants as to the traveller, if a bridge of one arch were to be thrown over the Tavey, like that of Pont y Pridd which from the steepness of the banks of the river might easily be effected in such a manner that vessels might pass under it with all their sails standing. I had the satisfaction in my second tour, that such an undertaking had been in contemplation, but that it was not yet begun, from the violent opposition of the parties. Swansea makes a handsome appearance from the approach to it being built near the mouth of the Tavey, on a semicircular rising bank above it. It carries on considerable trade in coals, pottery and copper. A large copper works is perpetually smoaking within view of the town, and another, still larger employs many hands. The plenty of coals in this neighbourhood, and the convenience of exportation, have induced the copper companies to fix on this spot.

Such indeed is the profusion of lime-stones and coals in Glamorganshire, that lime is the general manure of the whole country. The houses, walls and outbuildings are commonly whitewashed and there is scarcely a cottage to be seen, which is not regularly brushed every month.

31. Wyndham, H. P. A Tour of Monmouthshire and Wales. G. Wilkie, London. pp. 36-7.

ORIGIN OF THE WELSH

The origin of every nation is necessarily obscure and always lost in antiquity. On the authority of Bochart we may trace the Welsh from Japhet, son of Noah.

32. Romantic. A Collection of Welsh Tours, Introduction. G. Sael, 1797, p. 134.

MR MORRIS'S COAL MINE

Swansea is a town of considerable importance in this part of Wales. It is remarkable for the convenience it affords to bathers, being almost equal to Weymouth in its white sands and beautiful shore. Many officers on half-pay, invited by the cheapness of provisions, make this town their place of residence.

We went one day to a public breakfast at the bathing house, and were agreeably surprised by seeing the company stand up to dance as soon as the tables were removed. This is an established custom, and we found it a very pleasant scheme. All was mirth and good humour; the harp struck up with a violin. I jumped up, as if by instinct, seized upon the sprightly daughter of an ironmonger and footed it away in my boots like the rest of the company, nor did we conclude our pastime until the room became empty.

A few days after our arrival we hired an open chaise, and drove to Mr Morris's coal mine. The method of exploring these subterranean caverns, is here rendered far more pleasant and expedient than those we visited in Cornwall.

The entrance is vaulted, and perfectly level, and continues so for about one hundred yards, when our guides made us turn off to the right, to a sort of staircase, which they call the horse road. By this we descended to a depth of eighty fathoms, and came to a spacious area, where the miners were sending up the coal in baskets through a shaft, to the vaulted level we had just quitted. It is there put into carts, with friction wheels, and drawn by oxen to the mouth of the mine.

It is pleasing to see the ease and quickness with which these amazing works are carried on. If a stranger beholds the dark passage by which the horses descend, who bring the coal from the place where it is dug to the shaft, he would be astonished, and unable to conceive how these animals can be taught to practise, without stumbling, and with facility, what he with care and attention, would find it difficult to perform. Proceeding onwards we came to some miners, who were engaged in blowing up part of the rock with gun powder, in order to make the communication from one part of the mine to another. Still farther onward, about half a mile from the entrance, we came to the cutters, as they are called, a troop of miserable black devils, working away their very lives amidst sulphur, smoke and darkness.

As you creep among these regions of darkness the guide who precedes you, calls out, every now and then desiring you to stand close. This happens when a load of coal is coming along the passage, which is heard at a distance, and if you stand close to the side, you are sure to be safe.

The wheels are placed on the iron bars, which they receive in a groove, and these bars being continued parallel to each other, they serve both as a guide to the cart and by lessening the friction, greatly diminish the weight of the load.

It is curious to see one of these carts pass. They are drawn by horses, and if they are empty, the driver lays along in them, seizing his beast by the tail, which serves him as a rein to guide the animal round the different turnings and windings in the passages.

One beautiful spectacle, however we had the luck to meet with, on our return from Melincourt to Swansea, and it came the more grateful as it was unexpected. This arose from the smelting houses which in the middle of a heavy rain, and a dark night, displayed such a glorious light and so many beautiful colours from their ashes which lay on each side of the road, that I should not have regretted being wet through, if it was for the pleasure of seeing these.

I was looking from the window of our inn on a Sunday evening, when suddenly I perceived an uncommon throng of people gathering in the street. A hearse, with the body of a young man, was moving towards the church. My companion was eager to see the funeral, and we both ran to attend the ceremony. The crowd was amazing. From the gate of the churchyard to the church door, we had as much difficulty in forcing our way, as we ever found in gaining admittance to the theatre on a benefit night. Women screaming, children crying, men swearing, dogs howling, cats squalling, formed a scene, of all others, the most unlike a funeral. The doors were at last opened, in we rushed and happy was he who could maintain his legs. The church became instantly filled, but what became of the body, or the clergyman, I never could discover.

Thus ended this motley specimen of Cambrian interment. I have heard many strange things of the Welsh and expect many more. 'Their name,' they say, 'liveth for ever more,' but of all their eccentricities, I defy any one to say of them, that 'their bodies are buried in peace.'

33. Clarke, E. D. A Tour through the South of England and Wales and part of Ireland. Minerva Press. 1791. pp. 195-202. 208-9.

SECTARIES VARIOUS

Our walk to Swansea was 8 miles by the inner road: the country between that and Neath is very rich and extremely well cultivated — the cottages and hamlets all white. We noticed as we walked several chapels spread over the country, and we knew that in this particularly the sectaries were various: but it is true, Madam, that Jumpers are so called, because when any one of them from fancied inspiration sees the Saviour, and springs up to touch Him, that the whole assembly in the same manner strive who shall first lay hold of the feet or the robes of the Lord? or that person who wishes to be initiated among them, be the sex or age what it may, is immersed as if on the borders of Jordan? I hope, on my return to London, you will fix my opinion as to these circumstances.

Before we got to Swansea we saw immense forges at work, and I could not enough admire the genius and oeconomy which transport copper hither, out of Cornwall in order to be wrought, coals being the principal production of this country, wh. is wanting in the other. Swansea feels greatly the advantage of this commerce; by its situation it is, as it were, the staple town between the interior country of Wales, and the opposite coast of England, particularly Bristol. Company also frequents Swansea for the advantage of the sea bathing, and I have heard say, that it would be a place of great resort if the Bathing were better conducted: but, notwithstanding this, and though on the great road to Ireland, there is but one decent inn, the master of which is not backward in taking due advantage of such a circumstance. We had heard Swansea very highly spoken of — without doubt this town is agreeably situated at the bottom of an immense Bay, open to the South and East, and from its being built at the foot of a mountain, entirely screened from the North Wind.

34. Pedestrian Traveller. Letters describing a tour through part of Wales. Edwards, Pall Mall. 1797. p. 42.

WALTER SAVAGE LANDOR

W. S. Landor 1775-1864.
Removed from Rugby at Headmaster's request and privately educated.
Trinity College, Oxford. 1793.
Rusticated for shooting at the windows of a Tory opponent.
Refused to return.
Exiled on an allowance of £150 from 1793-7 in S. Wales.
Met Nancy Jones in Tenby and lived with her in Swansea with their daughter.
Met, on the burrows at Swansea, in October 1796, Rose, only

daughter of the 4th Baron Aylmer and Catherine Whitworth, and step-daughter of Howel Price of Laugharne.

I am not insensible to what is generally taken to be expressed, in matters of literature as in many other things by popularity. The writer whom crowds of readers wait upon has deserved his following, be it for good or ill: and the desire to read without the trouble of thinking, which railways have largely encouraged and to which many modern reputations are due, has not prevented the growth of other reputations that will outlive the contemporaries who conferred them.

But with this popular literature which in some form always exists, there has existed at all times a literature less immediately attractive but safer from caprice or vicissitude, finding its audiences, fit however few, the same through the ages. Its principal masters have been the men who have from time to time purified enlarged and refined the language: who have gathered to it new possessions, extending its power and variety. They have left unsatisfied the eager wish for the sensational or merely pleasurable on whose gratification popularity so much depends: and they have never had for their audience those multitudes of readers who cannot wait to consider and enjoy. Taking rank with this rare class is the writer, Walter Savage Landor.

It is not my intention to speak otherwise than frankly of his character and of his books. Though I place him in the first rank as a writer of English prose: though he was a genuine poet: and there is no exaggeration in the saying of one of his American admirers (J. Russell Lowell of Boston) that, excepting Shakespeare, no other writer has furnished us with so many or so delicate aphorisms of human nature: his faults lie more upon the surface than is usual with writers of this high order.

It was unfortunate for him in his early years that self control was not necessarily forced on a temperament which had peculiar need of it; and its absence affected both his books and life disastrously.

He was born at Warwick, the son of a doctor of good family, educated at Rugby and Oxford from which he was sent down after a shooting incident. He was finally given an allowance and spent the next three years almost wholly at Tenby and Swansea.

That this interval could not in any prudent or worldly sense have been very profitable to him, what has been said will sufficiently have shown . . .

One thing nevertheless is to be said of these three years, that in the course of them his mind passed through a discipline which from previous studies or emotions it had failed to acquire; that during them he appears to have read more steadily and persistently than at any former time; and that he printed at the close of them, when he had scarcely passed his twentysecond year, a poem which has only hitherto wonderfully attracted the few as it has decisively repelled the many, but which in my judgement is yet sure of taking admitted rank, if not in this, in some other generation, with those few productions of the highest class which contain writing that will perish only with the language.

'When I began to write Gebir, I had just read Pindar a second time and understood him. What I admired, was what nobody else had noticed, his proud complacency and scornful strength. If I could resemble him in nothing else I was resolved to be compendious and exclusive.' Besides Pindar he read again Homer and the Tragedians: and what for the purpose in hand was far more important he had finally laid aside Pope and betaken himself to Milton.

'My prejudices in favour of ancient literature began to wear away on Paradise Lost and even the great hexameter sounded to me tinkling when I had recited aloud, in my solitary walks on the seashore, the haughty appeal of Satan and the repentance of Eve.'

In such walks for the most part and under such influences Gèbir was composed: and it was probably no illusion of his fancy which led him to say in after life that he was never happier than when thus writing it, and not exchanging twelve sentences with men. Copper works had not as yet, quite filled the woods around Swansea among which he lived; and he might take his daily walks, as he has himself described them, over sandy sea-coast deserts covered with low roses only and thousands of nameless flowers and plants, and with nothing save occasional prints of the naked feet of the Welsh peasantry to give token of any human creatures. Hardly human indeed, in the savagery in those days, were the lower orders of the Welsh. The English visitor might have some excuse for regarding them as only something a very little higher than animals.

They were as much mere adjuncts to his landscape as its stranded boats or masses of weeds.

The accident which led him to Gebir I have often heard him relate. He was on friendly terms with some of the family of Lord Aylmer, who were staying in the neighbourhood, and one of the young ladies lent him a book, by a now forgotten writer of romances, from the Swansea circulating library. Clara Reeve was the author; but Landor, confusing in his recollection a bad romance writer with a worse of the same sex, thought it was that sister of Mrs Siddons and John Kemble who lived in the small Welsh town, and wrote under the name of Anne of Swansea. Few of my readers will have heard her name and I may warn them against all her books.

35. Forster, John. Walter Savage Landor, Chapman and Hall, London. 1869 pp. 2, 77, 132, 133.

O for the spirit of that matchless man
Whom Nature led throughout her whole domain
While he, embodied, breathed ethereal air !
Tho' panting in the play hour of my youth
I drank of Avon too, a dangerous draught,
That roused within the feverish thirst of song.

36. Landor, W. S., Gebir and other poems, Moxon, London. 1831. p. 380.

A young lady of great beauty and accomplishments, Rose was only seventeen when he met her and Landor, who had been living more or less openly with a mistress, was in no position to make honourable advances. Without her brother's formal permission to pay his addresses he could not offer words of love, but he probably showed his attraction, waxing sentimental as was his instinctive habit with women, and since she welcomed his company, he had reason to suppose she was not indifferent to him. Their acquaintance lasted only eighteen months, for in the summer of 1798 Rose accompanied her aunt, the wife of Sir John Henry Russell, when she went out to India to join her husband, a Bengal judge. There she died of cholera in 1800 and the news of her death inspired Landor to write the best-known lines of all his verse.

Ah! what avails the sceptred race!
Ah! what the form divine!
What every virtue, every grace!
Rose Aylmer, all were thine.
Rose Aylmer, whom these wakeful eyes
May weep, but never see.
A night of memories and of sighs
I consecrate to thee.

36. Landor, W. S., Simonidea. In: Gebir and other poems.

NOTE. The poem was first called St. Clair and did not include the name of Rose Aylmer in the original version. It bore the date of their first meeting, October 5, 1796.

Many things I had to say to you which there was not time for. One why should I forget? 'Tis for Rose Aylmer which has a charm I cannot explain. I lived upon it for weeks.

37. Lamb, Charles. Letter to Landor.

According to his brother Robert, Landor lived with Nancy Jones at Swansea till the birth of their child. It seems unlikely that the connection lasted long after this meeting with Rose Aylmer, which happened about the same time as the burial of the nine month's child at Swansea. Nancy herself died in 1801.

On the dead

And thou too, Nancy! why should Heaven remove
Each tender object of my early love?
Why was I happy? O ye conscious rocks!
Was I not happy? When Ione's locks
Claspt round her neck and mine their golden chain
Ambition, fame, and fortune smiled in vain.
Tho' Nancy's name forever dwell unknown
Beyond her briar-bound sod and upright stone
Yet, in the lover's, in the poet's eye
The gentle young Ione ne'er shall die.

36. From Gebir and other poems.

Child of a day, thou knowest not
The tears that overflow thy urn
The gushing eyes that read thy lot
Nor, if thou knewest, couldst return.
And why the wish! the pure and blest
Watch like thy mother o'er the sleep.
O peaceful night; O envied rest!
Thou wilt not ever see her weep.

38. Ibid.

THE MUMBLES RAILWAY

How beautiful was the sea shore covered with low roses, yellow snapdragons, and thousands of other plants. That streak of black along the most beautiful coast in the universe will never succeed in rendering me indifferent to Swansea. Two years afterwards the detestable tram road was made along it. Besides, before this, thousands of small vessels covered the bay, laden with lime and whatever else is now carried in those train wagons. The Gulf of Salerno, I hear, is much finer that Naples, but give me Swansea for scenery and climate. I prefer good apples to bad peaches. If it should ever be my fortune, which I cannot expect, and do not much hope, to return to England, I pass the remainder of my days in Swansea — between that place and Mumbles. Nothing but the education and settlement of my children would make me at all desirous of seeing England again.

Landor, W. S. Letter to his mother, from Italy. See 39.

NOTE. Because of constant difficulties, especially over Llanthony Abbey, Landor quitted England.

Though a packet of hair was found in his desk after his death it was not Ione's 'once mingled with my own' but Rose Aylmer's.

39. Elwin, Malcolm. Walter Savage Landor. Macmillan & Co. 1941. pp. 36, 58.

FASHIONABLE SWANSEA

Swansea, both in extent, the width of its streets and the aspects of its buildings, far exceeds all the towns in South Wales; it has of late been greatly improved; though its principal consequence is derived from its increasing commerce, it owes much to the mildness of its climate and the singular beauty of the bay it commands. These advantages, together with a commodious shore for sea-bathing, have made it the resort of that gay tribe of company which embellishes the public places of the coast of England, as well the winter residence of many families from the frequented parts of South Wales. A theatre and an assembly room contribute to the general amusement and all the resources of polished society are here at times to be found amidst the noise of manufactures and the buzz of incessant commerce.

The remains of Swansea Castle consist chiefly of a massy tower with a curious light parapet upon Gallic arches; this castle and that of Oystermouth were built by Henry Beaumont, earl of Warwick, in the reign of Henry I. Oystermouth is a very fine ruin on the coast, at a distance of about four miles from Swansea, near the promontory of the Mumbles Head, which terminating in high hills, and stretching far out into the bay, affords a safe anchorage to ships passing up and down the channel.

This headland of Mumbles forms a point of the peninsula of Gower which extends in a long and narrow isthmus between the two great bays of Glamorganshire and Carmarthenshire; this is in general a rocky and uninteresting district, except where the sea views enliven it! Yet has fancy, or some other cause of predilection disposed Mr Talbot to create a highly ornamented villa, with all its luxurious appendages, at Penrice, near the extremity of the tract, where the castles of Penrice and Pennarth, built soon after the Conquest, distinguish the bay of Oxwich. The house is an elegant modern structure, and the diversities of lawn, wood, and water, introduced with much taste and design, strongly contrast with the asperities of the surrounding district; and surprise a stranger with a degree of refinement he could little expect in such a tract. Yet may an observer, without too critic an eye, deem the trim aspect of this park, and its smooth sheet of water, inconsonant with the rough outline of the coast and country; and censure that design which has introduced the principal approach through fictitious fragments of a modern ruin, within sight of an ancient castle, whose ivied walls overhanging the beach, seem to frown defiance at this newly created rival. Still more must he wonder, that its owner should desert the noble seat of Margam, in the midst of a populous and plentiful country, to form a fairy palace in a dreary and desolate wild, far from the usual haunts of men, and near the extremity of a bleak peninsula.

40. Skrine, J. H. Two succesive tours throughout the whole of Wales. Emsley and Bremner, 1798. pp. 68 et seqq.

NOTE. The Reverend J. H. Skrine of Teddington, Middlesex was later clerk to John Henry Vivian, of Marino, later Singleton Abbey.

INDUSTRIAL SWANSEA

Swansea being a fashionable bathing place, we judged it necessary to make as smart an appearance there as the situation of our wardrobes would allow; having therefore brushed up at a small village, about a mile from the town and hired a lad to carry our knapsacks, we boldly proceeded to the Mackworth Arms, the best inn in the place. Pride, however, generally punishes itself; and fortune, who had always hitherto rewarded our ebbullitions of vanity with shame and confusion of face, determined not to lose this opportunity of exerting her malignity. While we were hastening to the inn, affecting that stare of conscious importance which a seat in a phaeton and four will hardly authorise, a cry from behind attracted our attention. Looking around we beheld our poor page prostrate in the gutter, the packs rolling away from him in different directions and mine, which was stuffed beyond its capacity of extension, burst from top to bottom, discharging its heterogeneous contents over the pavement and converting the streets into a second ragfair. I verily believe the smiles of some smart girls, who were taking their afternoon promenade, and the unrestricted mirth of half a dozen sailors would have put our party to flight had not John, whose practical philosophy is equal to his invincible good humour persuaded us to collect together the different articles by observing that it is much better to suffer the transient ordeal of a little ridicule and endure the evaporation of a little self importance, than run the risque of losing the contents of the knapsack. Common sense seconded his remark, and in a few minutes we had secured our property, and were safely lodged in the Mackworth Arms.

The whole of this day has been employed in surveying Swansea and ascertaining some facts relative to its trade and population. Situated at the mouth of the River Tawe, (and thence called Abertawe in Welsh) in the centre of a deep and secure bay, it possesses such important advantages as have rendered it the most considerable seaport in the principality. Lofty hills defend it on the north-east and north-west. The Bristol Channel spreads itself in front, bounded by the high cliffs of Somersetshire, and the rich beautiful and diversified coast of Glamorganshire shuts it in to the right and left.

The town is large and well built, containing a population (rapidly increasing) of nearly seven thousand; the houses, chiefly modern, handsome and commodious. Two expensive breweries, roperies, a fine dry dock, and much ship-building, supply occupation for a great number of workmen. Its trade chiefly consists in the exportation of stone coal, iron ore and limestone, all found on the banks of the Tawe, and brought to Swansea by canal. Of the first of these articles about a hundred thousand cauldrons (thirty six bushels to the cauldron) are usually shipped from the port for foreign markets, as well as home consumption. Seven large copper houses, also, at a small distance from the town, smelting annually forty five thousand tons of this metal, and consuming seventy thousand chaldrons of coal, find employment for many coasting vessels, which bring ore from Cornwall and Anglesey, and load back with coal and culm. Added to these sources of wealth and importance, Swansea enjoys a part of the Baltic and West India commerce, which, united with its home trade, have so swelled its commercial consequence as to put it nearly on a level with Bristol, in respect to tonnage, and superior to it with regard to the number of vessels that visit its quays.

The rapid increase in trade made by this place (notwithstanding the check which war has naturally produced) in the course of a few years will best be understood by the following view extracted from the custom-house books here:—

In the year 1768 there entered at Swansea 694 vessels.

1794 1757 „ 105007 tons

1795	1787	,,	112907	,,
1796	1741	,,	103560	,,
1797	1897	,,	115045	,,
$\frac{3}{4}$/1798	1558	,,	94704	,,

The beauty of its situation, and its admirable bathing accommodation have rendered Swansea the resort of many respectable families of South Wales during the summer season: and an excellent hotel has been erected there within these few years, near to the sea for their reception.

Here a fine hard sand stretches away to the South-east embracing within its sweeping recesses the waters of Swansea Bay, and commanding the enchanting scenery of the Glamorganshire coast.

Even now, my dear sir, am I returned from pacing this sandy level, and watching, for the last time, the full-orb'd sun slowly sinking into the western wave. The evening calm and serene; the face of the deep, smooth and tranquil; the distant hills melting into thin air, and from the ling'ring tints of day fading gradually from the summits of the opposite rocks, formed a picture that irresistibly impelled the mind to serious reflection, and produced a natural question in my bosom, whether the wonders, the glories and the beauties of nature, which had displayed themselves during our tour, had in any degree improved my heart as well as interested my imagination.

Accuse me not of vanity, if I tell you the answer was such as gave rise to a hope that they have not been altogether unproductive of improvement; that I shall return from an expedition extremely pleasurable, with an increase of humility, and expansion of benevolence and an enlargement of every better affection; and bid adieu (though with regret) to the shores of Cambria, if not a wiser, at least a better man than when I first visited them, with no wish at my heart but the rational aspiration of the poet.

'Farewell thy printless sands and pretty shore!
I hear the white surge beat thy coast no more!
Pure, gentle source of the high rapt'rous mood
Where'er like the great flood, by thy dread force
Heav'n Earth and Ocean's Lord. And Father of the Good!

41. Warner, Rev. Richard. A second walk through Wales. 1799. C. Dilly, Poultry, London. pp. 360 et seqq.

THE NEW PIER

Swansea is a borough town, consisting of a portreeve, recorder, twelve aldermen, two common attornies or chamberlains, and an unlimited number of burgesses; and together with six contributory boroughs sends a member to parliament. Swansea being the chief town in the county, not only on account of its charming situation, and extensive trade, but the beauty of its neighbourhood, it is presumed the following attempt at a methodical account of what may be thought worthy of observation, will be deemed useful to the curious or inquisitive traveller.

From a bird's eye view best seen from the round Tower of the Castle or Kilvey Hill, the whole town is brought into a distant and beautiful perspective, forming an irregular oblong figure nearly a mile and a half in length, and finely intersected by the meanders of the river, receiving into its mouth the numerous shipping and craft which constitute its wealth and support its consequence.

The bay is universally allowed to be singularly beautiful and the shore very commodious for bathing; as the great influx of company for many years for that purpose sufficiently evince. The town in consequence has undergone many capital improvements; and the new Pier, as it is of admirable advantage to the harbour of Swansea, so it is, with the adjoining Burrows, a most pleasant promenade, comprehending much pleasant scenery.

The Burrows contain many good lodging houses, pleasantly situated; and that of Mr Jordan's in particular is fitted up with an excellent Warm Sea-Water Bath, on the following terms:—

> *Bathing each time three shillings, each napkin if found by the proprietor two pence, with an additional sixpence for bathing in the winter half year. Near which stands an elegant chapel built in the year 1789, used by the followers of Lady Huntingdon; the present minister is the Reverend Mr Kemp.*

Wind Street is handsome and well paved; at one end of which is the Look-out, the Custom-house, the Circulating Library (Mr Oakey's) opposite to which is the Post-Office, and the Glamorgan Bank of Messrs Landeg and Co. . The Mackworth Arms, kept by Lewis Rotely, a good house, admirably adapted for the accom-

Temple Street with Theatre and 'Three Lamps'

Wind Street

CLASEMONT P. F. BOURGEOIS 1782

LANDORE WITH ' MORRIS CASTLE ' J. C. IBBETSON 1792

ARTHUR'S STONE GASTINEAU

PENRICE CASTLE DUGDALE

View of the Copper Works and Morriston

J. G. Wood 1811

Tram Bridge over the Tawe I. G. Wood 1811

Bristol Copper Works I. G. Wood 1811

THE TAWE FERRY

BATHING HUTS 1841

Swansea Pier

Venus a la Coquelle (Ann of Swansea)

modation of the more stilish traveller: at some distance is the Market place for corn, fish and vegetables: the house is said to be covered with the lead of St. David's given by Cromwell to a gentleman of the town: on the left is Butter Street or rather St. Mary's where the greater share of the market is held for butcher's meat, poultry, butter, etc., on the right stands the more perfect part of the old Castle, now used as a gaol and workhouse. This Castle, which must once have been very extensive, was burnt by Griffin, prince of South Wales, and was probably built by Henry the 1st, about 1113, when he fortified the town; the small arches round the top of it are exactly similar to the building of Lanphy Castle and King John's Hall, St. David's Pembrokeshire. Near the Castle is the old Mansion of the Lords of the Manor, built round a quadrangle; over the gate the Arms of William, Earl of Pembroke, Henry VIII, quartering Sir George Herbert, lord of Swansea. Joining the Castle is the more modern-built Town-Hall length fifteen yards by six. Near which is built the new Market, built in 1774, commodious in every respect, and where a lesser weekly market on Wednesday is held.

Worcester Place consists of a range of neat houses the chief of which is the residence of Thomas Morgan, Esq., the present portreeve and proprietor of the whole row.

Between the Market place and the Higher Town is Castle Bailey or Castle Bailiwick street, divided in the middle by a straight line of stones ranged longitudinally, and so denominated, because that part or division next the Castle is within the verge or bailiwick of the Court and secures the person confined for debt, and who having leave of the bailiff for the limits of the court, does not exceed the bounds, from any arrest or further molestation.

In the vicinity of Swansea, one mile west is St. Helen's, the seat of John Jones, Esq., captain in the service of the Hon. East India Company. A mile farther is Marino, a curious octagonal building, the tasty retirement of Edward King, Esq., built by Mr Jernigan.

Swansea canal has no less than thirty-six locks in the space of fifteen miles.

42. Oldisworth, Rev. J. First Swansea Guide. Z. B. Morris, Swansea. 1802.

pp. 6-10, 49, 59.

NOTE. The Rev. J. Oldisworth was Master of Bishop Gore's School in Goat Street.

POOR SERVICE

The sea being out we proceeded over the sands, under Kilvey Hill, and ferrying over the Tawy, entered the town of Swansea; the faculties more awake when abroad, circumstances strike, which perhaps would pass unnoticed at home. In the street our attention was called by a shrill voice, an octave higher than is usual on such occasions, delivering a story of considerable length. Hastening to the spot we found it was the crier of the town, a female, announcing to the public the arrival of a cargo of goods, which were then selling on the quay for ready money. Whether this appointment was made in compliment to the sex, or the corporation might think the office would be more ably filled, I know not, but the circumstance of a herault femelle did not fail to excite the risibility of the party.

Situated in a most charming bay, in an angle between two hills on the north western bank of the Tawy, the town is defended from the chilling blasts; and the south wind coming over an expanse of water renders the air mild; and the soil for the most part sand or gravel, the place must naturally be congenial to health. It is called by the Welsh Aber Tawy. Its present name is derived according to Camden, from the number of porpoises frequenting the bay; as if Swein or Swine-sea. By others from the smoothness of the waters in the bay, as if Swansea. Might I hazard a conjecture, I should suppose it formerly called Swang-sea, from Swang an old word signifying a green sand or marsh, sometimes overflowed; and the traces that the present bay was once a wood, numbers of stools of large trees being yet visible, would lead to such a conjecture.

It is the wish of the inhabitants, that Swansea should be viewed in the light of a fashionable resort, rather than as a trading town; and a bathing place, rather than a seaport. Numerous houses are fitted up as lodgings for those disposed to visit this maritime spot, and some in the Burrows (destroyed, November 1795 by high tide) are neat and pleasant, commanding a view both of the river and the bay. But the distance from the only situation eligible for the machines being more than a mile, renders these inconvenient for valetudinarians. The corporation therefore, were induced to erect a large building near the spot, for the further accommodation of the delicate, called the bathing-house. The view from hence includes the bay and parts of the surrounding country and the assembly room forms a pleasing promenade for the company at the house in unfavourable weather.

You will suppose I am got into a fashionable place like Weymouth, surrounded by the blandishments of gaiety and pleasure; but descriptions sometimes lead to wrong estimates.

If we enter into a comparison between this place and the favourite spot of the Royal Family, it must be made by a list of negatives. No hot rolls and delicate pats of butter salute you in the morning; no crabs, lobsters, prawns, and other delicious fish at dinner; no gentle airings to Wick and Upway; no parties to the romantic beauties of Lulworth Cove, no aquatic excursions, to hear the beautiful effect of music on the water, while the royal band is playing on the Esplanade. No public breakfasts, and dancing to the sound of pipe and tabor, on the green; no regattas or frequent military reviews; no balls on board frigates, and dining on board men of war. In short after stating that there is a tolerable sandy beach, machines indifferently kept, dressing rooms for the sick, and lodgings for those in health, the rest must be imagined, not experienced. No horses, no carriages, no pleasure boats. You may sometimes, by great exertion and persuasion, induce the idle fellows, as a particular favour to go out. But such is their fear, that they never venture far; and such is their unskillfullness that more than one instance has occurred of the party being swamped.

A total inattention to the comforts and conveniences of the company is manifest in those most interested in the concern: and a perfect apathy to the manifold blessings procurable by exertion too evidently exists among the inhabitants of Swansea. It has been pronounced the most complete bathing place in the kingdom, but whether this is not a more interested than accurate account, I leave for decision to those who may have opportunities of ascertaining the fact.

43. Evans, Rev. John. Letter written during a tour through South Wales. Baldwin. 1804. pp. 159, 160, 164, 168.

NELSON AND THE HAMILTONS IN SWANSEA

At Swansea the party were the guests of John Morris at Clasemont and from here they visited the places of local interest; the Cambrian Pottery managed by Lewis Weston Dillwyn, later to produce and market a remarkably fine porcelain which achieved such considerable success, was one of the first places they saw. They inspected the pier and harbour also and one wonders if Sir William who was so well qualified to do it, echoed the thoughts of the poet Walter Savage Landor, a frequent visitor to this coast and who declared that its sweeping bay with the hills rising behind, 'outrivalled the claims of the Bay of Naples.' Certainly if he climbed the heights above Margam during the party's visit the following day, he could not fail to have made this favourable comparison. It was Walter Savage Landor, who also wrote:

Gone are the sirens from their sunny shore,
The muses afterwards were heard no more,
But of the Graces there remains but one —
Gods name her Emma, mortals, Hamilton.

In Swansea town the birthplace of an equally celebrated character Beau Nash, again the populace took over, and here there were a number of sailors on leave, who drew one of the open carriages through the streets much to everyone's delight. When they reached Wind Street, they were joined by more sailors, including the licensee of the Plume and Feathers, one Tom Cleaves: he had formerly been a boatswain on one of Nelson's vessels and was intimately known to his Lordship. Jostling to a position near the carriage, Cleaves with his boatswain's pipe in hand, blew three distinct and peculiar blasts on his whistle. At the sound of this, Lord Nelson sprang from his seat and turned to face the crowd exclaiming, 'Tom Cleaves' pipe by Jove!' and calling the carriage to a stop, shook the bo's'n warmly by the hand.

On Monday the freedom of the borough was presented to Lord Nelson and Sir William, and his Lordship made a short speech in which he expressed his heartfelt gratification and thanks for so honourable a testimony of his conduct. The bells of all the churches rang out 'for the hero of the age, the restorer of peace and plenty,' and Nelson gave two guineas for the Swansea Ringers.

44. Freeman, E. C. and Gill, E.; Johns, Newport, 1962. pp. 27-8.

On or about August 13th, 1802, Lord Nelson, who was then making a tour through Monmouthshire and South Wales, visited Swansea. Sir William and Lady Hamilton were of the party, and on the following day a banquet was given by the Portreeve in honour of the occasion. It is said that Lady Hamilton at the conclusion of the banquet sang popular airs such as, 'God Save the King' and 'Rule Britannia' to the great delight of the audience. The freedom of Swansea was then presented to Nelson and to Sir William Hamilton. The entry in the borough records dated Saturday August 14th, 1802 reads: —

> *Resolved unanimously that the Right Honourable Horatio Nelson, Viscount Nelson of the Nile and of Burnham Court in the county of Norfolk, duke of Bronte in Sicily, Knight of the Bath, etc., be admitted a burgess of this borough — ditto the Right Honourable Sir William Hamilton, Knight of Bath.*

After the banquet an expedition was made to the harbour, pier and pottery. When visiting the pottery Nelson bathed in the public baths erected by the Coles and Haynes shortly before 1798 on the Pottery premises. The party accepted the invitation of John Morris, Esquire, of Clasemont to dinner, the carriage being drawn through the streets of Swansea, to quote the Cambrian, by a choice body of tars, exulting in the happiness and glory they had in showing their respect to one of their own body, The Hero of the Age and the Restorer of Peace and Plenty.

45. Nance, E. M.: The Porcelain of Swansea and Nantgarw. Batsford, 1942. pp. 83-4

Join we great Nelson's name,
First on the roll of fame,

Him let us sing,
Spread we his praise around,
Honour of British ground,
Who made Nile's shores resound,
God save the King.

Verses sung by Lady Hamilton to 'God Save the King.'

NOTE.
Emma Hamilton c. 1765-1815, born Lyon, of Great Neston, Cheshire.
Married Sir William Hamilton (1730-1803) in Sept. 1791.
Inherited an income of £800 p.a. from Sir William's Welsh estates which had belonged to his first wife, Katherine Barlow of Lawrenny, an heiress. Emma died in poverty abroad.

Horatio Nelson 1758-1805
Left his wife in 1800 and lived with the Hamiltons.

THE CAMBRIAN POTTERY

Gentlemen, I shall be very happy to receive your pottery and if you will have the goodness to tell me who to pay the bill to in London, it shall be done. I hope this service will be of use to the infant manufactory. I am, Gentlemen, with many thanks for your kind attention in showing me your works, your most obliged, humble servant,

Nelson and Bronte.

My dear Sir James Fellowes, like his own Western Sun, delights to warm and gild the evening of a stormy day; but I have no commissions that I can remember. Divi Robinson has sent the wire and I have sent the money, so that's all over. When you feel your purse too heavy, take it to Mortlock's in Oxford Street, and carry Lady Fellowes a beautiful specimen of South Wales china and tell him I am panting for my ice pails and large dishes to use this day se'night.

Yours and all the family's obliged,
Hester Lynch Piozzi. 1810

46. As Mrs Thrale, a great friend of Samuel Johnson.

BOUND TO SWANSEA

In company with another artist, I entered Bristol with an intention of commencing my Cambrian tour in the neighbourhood of Chepstow; but an unthought-of attraction induced us to relinquish this project. Returning from a ramble through the town, by the quay, we were agreeably amused with a fleet of vessels that was about to quit the river with the ebbing tide; some of them were already in full sail floating down the stream, and others getting under weigh. The spirited exertions of the seamen, and the anxious movements of numerous spectators, devoting their attention to friends or freight, gave animation to the scene, which was rendered particularly cheerful by the delightful state of the morning. On a sudden we were saluted with a duet of French-horns from a small sloop in the river; a very indifferent performance to be sure, yet it was pleasing.

Their sloop was bound to Swansea; and we learned that the wind was so directly favourable, that the voyage would in all probability be completed the same afternoon. We were now strongly disposed for an aquatic excursion; nor did the laughing broad faces of about a dozen Welch girls, passengers, alarm us from our purpose: so by an exertion we collected our portmanteaus and some refreshments in due time, and engaged in the voyage.

For some time we were well entertained with our voyage; when satisfied with external objects, we found amusement in the cooped-up circle of our companions, and entered upon a general meal, without the assistance of knives or plates, with much good humour: nor was there lack of wit, if we might judge from the continued bursts of laughter that sallied on the occasion. But the scene presently changed: the wind, at first so favourable, shifted to the opposite point, increasing from a pleasant breeze to a fresh gale; the sun no longer played on the surface of the water; the sky became overcast, and 'the waves curved darkly against the vessel'. From the seamen, with looks of disappointment, we learned, that the prospect of a short voyage was at an end; and that, if the wind continued as it was, we might be kept at sea for several days: the badness of the weather increased towards evening, when a deluging rain came down, aggravated by a noisy old woman on board, who grated our ears with a horrible scream whenever a wave broke over the vessel, or a flash of lightning illuminated the scenery of the storm: filling up the intervals with the cheering narrative of ships that were lost in the very track of our voyage. It was to no purpose that we endeavoured to joke away her fears, or to make them less eloquent; but Time, that great resolver of difficulties, transferring the disorder to her stomach, quieted her alarm. At length the increasing rain forced every one for shelter towards the cabin: this was a hole about two yards by one and a half; not quite the latter dimension in height, and filthy to a degree that I shall not attempt to describe; into this place as many were squeezed as it could possibly contain.

Among our female companions were two genteel young Welch-women of considerable personal attractions, whose vivacity and good nature had essentially contributed to the entertainment of the day; one of these was peculiarly bewitching, her's was

the faultless form
Shap'd by the hand of harmony: the cheek
Where the live crimson, through the native white
Soft-shooting, o'er the face diffuses bloom,
And ev'ry nameless grace; the parted lip
Like the red rose-bud moist with morning dew
Breathing delight; and, under flowing jet,
The neck slight shaded, and the swelling breast,
The look resistless, piercing to the soul.

These damsels preferring the certainty of a wetting upon deck to the chance of suffocation in the cabin, we made it our business to defend them as much as possible from the pelting and pitiless storm. Our travelling coats were fashionably large; so that each of us was able completely to shelter one, without exposing our-selves; a bottle of brandy too, that we had fortunately provided, helped to counteract the inclemency of the weather, and we were for some time thoroughly comfortable. The rain at length, pene-trating our coverings, obliged us to seek a fresh resource; but to discover one was no easy matter; for the cabin had not a chink unoccupied, and there was not a dry sail on board to make use of. In this predicament it fortunately occurred to one of the ladies, that before the hatchway was closed she observed sufficient room in the hold for three or four persons who were not very bulky to lie down: to this place we gained admittance; and, although the angles of chests and packages formed a very inappropriate couch for the tender limbs of our friends, yet the retreat proved highly gratifying; and we enjoyed a refreshing sleep. — Unhallowed thoughts, be silent! voluptuous imaginations, conjure not up, from the pressure of circumstances, motives or actions that are unholy. It is true, the girls had charms that might warm an anchorite, and were filled with the glowing sensations of youthful passion; yet they were virtuous; nor had the tourists, although encountering temptation, a wish to endanger the possessors of qualities so lovely for a transistory enjoyment.

When we issued from our burrow the next morning the rain continued; but the wind abated, and became more favourable. The other passengers remained in the cabin, and nothing can be imagined more distressing than their situation. No less than ten women had squeezed themselves into the hole where they lay all of a heap, like fish in a basket. The heat and confinement had rendered the sickness general: I shall forbear to describe the evidence of its effects; but briefly remark, that, overcome by pain and fatigue, they appeared all in a sound sleep, half released from their clothes, and with such an intermixture of heads, bodies, and limbs, that it required some ingenuity to trace the relation of the several parts. The two old French-horn players were lying at the door, soaking in the rain, but also asleep. From such a scene we gladly withdrew, and in a few hours found ourselves at the entrance of Swansea Bay, finely encircled with high varied hills; on our left were two isolated rocks called the Mumbles, at a small distance from the mainland, where the whitened town of Ostermouth appeared issuing from the water, beneath a lofty dark hill. At the bottom of the bay, the superior extent of Swansea lined the shore backed by an atmosphere of cloudy vapours produced from the numerous furnaces in its neighbourhood. At length I trod on Cambrian ground, and paid my half crown, with a willing engagement to forfeit a hundred times the sum if ever I should be again caught on board a Swansea Hoy.

I obtained a complete survey of Swansea Castle (situated in the middle of the town), which, although much contracted from its former grand dimensions, is still of considerable extent. The principal feature of the building is, a massive quadrangular tower, remarkable for a range of light circular arches, encircling the top, and supporting a parapet, which forms a connexion with turrets at each angle . . . The tenantable parts comprise the town-hall; a poor-house; a jail; a new market house; numerous store-cellars; a blacksmith's and other shops and habitations; a Roman Catholic chapel; and a pigeon-house. The Gothic structure has been so far metamorphosed in its application to these purposes, that it is almost impossible to trace the original plan of the building; but the large apartment used for Romish worship has been either the baronial hall or the chapel: I think, the former . . .

Conspicuous above the other resorts of the manufacturers is Morristown, a neat newly-erected village; and on the summit of a steep hill Morristown Castle, a quadrangular building, which is the habitation of upwards of thirty families; these buildings owe their origin to Mr. Morris, a gentleman who, in partnership with Mr. Lockwood, conducts one of the leading works.

The introduction of Major Jones obtained me a view of Messrs Freeman's manufactory: we took care to be there at noon, when the furnaces are tapped and all the interesting processes gone through. The effect in passing through these dismal buildings, contrasted by the vivid glare of the furnaces and the lucid fire of the pouring metal, is to a stranger very striking. I was much surprised at the quantity of condensed sulphureous vapour that yellowed the roof of the building. Sulphur often forms the greatest bulk of the ore; yet no means are employed to collect the vapour, which might easily be managed, and could not fail of turning to a source of profit: at the same time, it would save the health of the workmen, and spare the vegetation, which appears stinted for a considerable distance by the noxious effluvia.

We left these sulphureous chambers to enjoy a purer air on the sea-shore, where another curiosity awaited us. As we were strolling on the sands, about a mile above the town, we remarked a group of figures, in birthday attire, gambolling in the water: not suspecting that they were women we passed carelessly on; but how great was our surprize, on approaching them, to find that the fact did not admit of a doubt. We had not paused a minute, before they all came running towards us, with a menacing tone and countenence, that would seem to order us away. Though we did not understand their British sentences, we obeyed, and very hastily too, on finding a volley of stones rattling about our ears. This hostile demonstration, we afterwards found, arose from a suspicion that we were going to remove their clothes, a piece of waggery often practised by the visitants of Swansea, to enjoy their running nudiores ovo. The girls knew we were not their countrymen, or we should have passed unconcerned; unless, indeed, acquaintances, who would have made their usual salutation, and perhaps joined in the party's amusement. In our subsequent rambles on the beach these liberal exhibitions of Cambrian beauty afforded us many pleasing studies of unsophisticated nature:

> Graceful, cleanly, smooth and round;
> All in Venus' girdle bound.

. . . . . .

From Pont-ar-dulais we had a pleasant ride to Swansea, where we rejoined a party of our friends at breakfast. During our stay in this town protracted to several days by its agreeable society, Mrs Hatton, mistress of the bathing house and sister of the English Melpomene exhibited her theatric powers on the humble boards of Swansea Theatre. But labouring under the misfortune of lameness, and the encumbrance of more human flesh than I ever before saw crowded in one female figure, she was obliged to go through her task, the recitation of Alexander's Feast, sitting; notwithstanding which weighty drawback, the lady did not fail to exhibit a vivid tincture of the family genius.

Here too we were gratified with the news of an event, before whose solid advantages the victories of a century sink, in a rational estimate, like glittering tinsel before massive ingots.

I was awakened at an early hour by the loud huzzas of the townspeople, and the frequent discharge of cannon from vessels in the harbour. The ships displayed their gayest colours; and the people, in dancing through the streets, congratulated each other on the long wished-for blessing of Peace! The chagrin of two or three provision-monopolizers, and a few others whose interest was in opposition to the public weal, with the old subterfuge that it was not the proper time for peace, covering a real sentiment of endless war, passed unnoticed, nor formed a perceptible speck on the brilliancy of the people's joy.

Our tour now took an eastward direction. Crossing Swansea river by an exceeding good ferry, and passing a region of furnaces, we traversed a considerable hill to the neighbouring valley of Neath.

47. Barber, J.T.: A Tour throughout South Wales and Monmouthshire, Cadell and Davies, 1803. pp. 14-27.

NOTE. The book is dedicated to Richard Brinsley Sheridan.

THE STONE OF SKETTY

From Pool dy Point it should be the object to keep along the seashore as much as possible to Oxwich Point, so as to have a complete view of Oxwich Bay, with its grand shores, caverns, and promontories. Penmaen is at the foot of a mountain, one of the highest in South Wales, on which there is a huge cromlech called in English King Arthur's Stone, and in Welsh the stone of Sketty. The lifting of this stone into its present place is mentioned in the Welsh historical triads as one of the three arduous undertakings accomplished in the island of Britain, and still more than that, as one of the three wonderful exertions of human power. The second was the erection of Stonehenge; and the third, the formation of a heap or pile, respecting which it cannot be discovered what, or where it was; but some have supposed that it might have been Silbury Hill, the vast tumulus near Marlborough. The immense stone in Gower is supported by several other stones.

Penrice Castle is the seat of Thomas Mansel Talbot, Esq., as I apprehend, of the Shrewsbury family. The house and grounds are much admired; but I cannot help testifying my surprise that Mr. Talbot, with such a subject to work upon, should not have worked differently. It is true that he has given all the elegance of Twickenham to a remote corner; has formed artificial pieces of water in front of Oxwich Bay; and built a modern villa, scarcely large enough for his own family, under the nodding towers of the ancient castle, which is converted into an aviary.

I have already mentioned the provincial red mantle, called a whittle, worn by the women of this district, and the people of Pembrokeshire; for they are the same people. Lady Mary Talbot generally wears a very fine mantle of this kind instead of a cloak, in precise fashion of the country, especially at church; and many other ladies, both here and in Pembrokeshire, are beginning to follow her example. I notice this little circumstance, because there seems to me to be both feeling, good sense and policy in persons of rank thus identifying themselves, if I may say so, with their neighbours and dependents.

A fine gothic window is nearly all that remains of Oxwich Castle. The village is remarkably neat and pretty, and well sheltered with wood. The cottages are in the comfortable style of Glamorganshire, with neat gardens, and what, I have observed nowhere else, every cottager has either a horse or a partnership in a horse, and his little hayrick in the garden, by the side of the house. The new parsonage house, built by Mr. Talbot as a testimony of respect to Mr Collins, the present rector, is beautifully situated on the beach, at the western side of the bay. The church is situated no less advantageously; and the point of land running out in to the channel at once protects the abodes of men and the works of vegetation against the destructive blasts of the Atlantic.

48. Malkin, Benjamin Heath. p. 489.

ANN OF SWANSEA

Great annoyance was caused to Sarah Siddons by the proceedings of her sister Ann who read lectures at Dr. Graham's Temple of Health, led a discreditable career, attempted to poison herself in Westminster Abbey, made appeals to the public, and announced herself everywhere as the youngest sister of Mrs Siddons. Mrs Siddons allowed her £20 a year on condition she lived 150 miles from London. Under the name of Hutton she wrote novels and was known as Ann of Swansea.

D.N.B.

Julia Ann Hatton 1764-1838.
Seventh child of Roger Kemble and Sarah Ward.
Married before 19 to an adventurer, Curtis, and deserted by him.
Married William Hatton in 1792 and went to America.
Leased Swansea Bathing House in 1799.

Moved to Kidwelly in 1806 on the death of Hatton and ran a dancing school.
Returned to Swansea in 1809 and lived on an annuity from P. J. Kemble.
Wrote a play, Zaffine, for Edmund Kean and, from 1815-1831, at least 12 novels.

D.W.B.

Buried at St. John's Church.

POETIC TRIFLES

Dedicated to the officers of the Royal Western Regiment of the Local Militia. It is not without apprehension Ann of Swansea sends her 'Poetic Trifles' into the world, in defence of which she takes the liberty of observing, that she has left no useful avocation — neglected no duties — to follow the allurements of the Muse.

SWANSEA BAY

In vain by various grief opprest
I vagrant roam devoid of rest
With aching heart, still ling'ring stray
Around the shores of Swansea Bay.

The restless waves that lave the shore
Joining the tide's tumultuous roar;
In hollow murmurs seems to say
Peace is not found at Swansea Bay.

The meek-eyed morning's lucid beam
The pensive moon's pale shadowy gleam,
Still ceaseless urge — why this delay?
Go, hapless wretch, from Swansea Bay.

'Tis not for me the snowy sail
Swells joyous in the balmy gale:
Nor cuts the boat with frolic play,
For me the waves of Swansea Bay.

The glow of health that tints each cheek,
The eyes that sweet contentment speak;
To mock my woes their charms display
And bid me fly from Swansea Bay.

Haste, smiling nymphs, your beauties lave
And sport beneath the sparkling wave,
While I pursue my lonely way,
Along the shores of Swansea Bay.

The foaming mountain's awful sweep
The rocks that beetle o'er the deep
The winds that round their summits play
All bid me fly from Swansea Bay.

Then Kilvey Hill, a long adieu
I drag my sorrows hence from you:
Misfortune, with imperious sway,
Impels mc far from Swansea Bay.

49. Hatton, Ann.: Poetic Trifles, John Bull, Waterford, 1811.

MARINO

In the immediate vicinity of Swansea, are several pleasant walks and objects, which we shall casually notice, before we take a few more distant excursions.

St. Helen's, the seat of Captain Jones lies about a mile to the westward; and a mile further is Marino, a curious octagonal building belonging to Edward King, esquire; near this is Verandah; and, at no great distance is Sketty Lodge, the residence of Mr Phillips, which, being on an eminence, commands the whole of Swansea Bay.

Across the river is Black-hill, Cline Wood, and the Woodlands, a house in the gothic style, belonging to Colonel Ward. Near the beach stands Lilliput Hall; which from the smallness of its dimensions, not ill deserves the title; but its accompaniments are so beautiful that the building is overlooked in the estimate which is formed of the place . . . And far up is the church of St. John's, now almost dilapidated.

50. Phillips, Richard: Watering and Sea bathing places. London 1810. p. 413.

NOTE. On August 21, 1784 Edward King, friend of Robert Morris, Barrister, leased Tir Powell from Mary Bevan, widow of Silvanus Bevan. It was part of the manor of East and West Millwood. The term was 21 years from 25th December 1783; rent £22 for the first 1½ years and £30 afterwards. Power was given to King to pull down the old farm and build a new messuage. (Marino). On March 23rd, 1805 a new lease was drawn up dating from 29th September, 1804 for the lives of the said Edward King and Jane his wife and for the life of the survivor. On 3rd February 1817, Edward King under-leased the premises to J. H. Vivian for 50 years if he (Edward King) should so long live, at a rent of £105.

J. H. Vivian bought or leased Veranda Lands, Mansion House and cottages; Cae ych Law yr rheol; Bryn (in 1828) and other land to form Singleton. Marino is partly incorporated in the former Singleton Abbey, now the University College of Swansea.

51. Rogers, W. C.: Swansea and Glamorgan Calendar, Part II, Vol. III. Swansea Public Library.

SHELLEY IN SWANSEA

On October 9th, Mary received an alarming letter and Shelley immediately set off for Bristol and Swansea. But the day preceding that of his arrival, October 10th, poor Fanny Imlay had committed suicide in the bedroom of an inn; a bottle of laudanum lay upon the table by her side, with a note which ran thus:

> *I have long determined that the best thing I could do was to put an end to the existence of a being whose birth was unfortunate, and whose life has only been a series of pain to the persons who have hurt their health in endeavouring to promote her welfare. Perhaps to hear of my death will give you pain; but you will soon have the blessing of forgetting that such a creature existed as . . .*

Mr. Dowden proves satisfactorily that Fanny's death cannot be attributed to an unfortunate attachment for Shelley as Claire asserts. Her letters, collected by Mr Dowden sufficiently explain her suicide, as being the natural result of excessive melancholy inherent in her disposition and increased by the nature of her surroundings in Skinner Street. (The Godwin home)

As Shelley read this last touching farewell, he recalled his last hurried interview with Fanny in London and penned the mournful stanza: —

Her voice did quiver as we parted,
Yet knew I not that heart was broken
From which it came, and I departed
Heeding not the words then spoken.
Misery — O Misery,
This world is all too wide for thee!

52. Rabbe, F.: Shelley, the man and poet. Ward & Downey, 1888. Vol. 2, pp. 80-1.

A melancholy discovery was made in Swansea yesterday: a most respectable looking female arrived at the Mackworth Arms on Wednesday night by the Cambrian Coach from Bristol: she took tea and retired to rest, telling the chambermaid she was exceedingly fatigued and would take care of the candle herself.

Much agitation was created in the house by her non-appearance yesterday morning, and on forcing her chamber door, she was found a corpse with the remains of a bottle of laudanum on the table and a note. The name appears to have been torn off and burnt, but her stockings are marked with letter G and on her stays the letters M.W. are visible. She was dressed in a blue striped skirt with a white body, and a brown pelice, with a fur trimming of a lighter colour, lined with white silk and a hat of the same. She had a small French gold watch, and appears about 23 years of age, with long brown hair, dark complextion and had a ridicule containing a red silk pocket handkerchief, a brown-berry necklace, and a small leather clasped purse containing three shillings and five shillings and six penny piece. She told a fellow traveller that she came from Bath by the mail from London on Tuesday morning from whence she proceeded to Bristol and from thence to Swansea by Cambrian coach. We hope the description we have given of this unhappy catastrophe will lead to the discovery of the wretched object who has prematurely closed her existence.

53. The Cambrian. Friday, October 11, 1816.

NOTE. Fanny was buried at St. John's Church, Swansea.

Gilbert Imlay, c. 1755, author and soldier. Captain in the American War of Independence. Published a Topographical Description of Western Territory of N. America in 1792 and the Emigrants, a novel, in 1793.
Lived at Le Havre and in London with Mary Wollstonecraft for 18 months. Left her in 1795 with a daughter, Fanny.

Mary Wollstonecraft. 1759-1797. Greatly in advance of her time. Married William Godwin in 1797 but died five months later giving birth to Mary Godwin, later Shelley.

William Godwin, 1756-1836, left with two young girls, later married a widow with family, living in Skinner Street, on reduced means.

TRAGEDY AT NANTGARW

My dear Sarah, Sept. 18th, 1817.

My sufferings are now arrived at the highest pitch of Misery, I lost on the first of January — My Dear Sarah — which my Dearest (now Departed) Lavinia wrote to you to state the event. But I have scarce calm'd a little my feelings for the loss of My Dear Sarah — than our Dearest Lavinia is taken from me, the only prop I had left to comfort and assist me in the great worldly sufferings I have to contend with. The Dearest Child was taken last Monday Morning with a violent pain in the Stomach and Bowels, I sent as soon as possible for a Doctor, it proved an Inflammation produc'd by a Cold caught the day before, every attention I could suggest and obtain for Her relief hath prov'd in Vain. In violent pain she continu'd but Much hopes of recovery I had and the Doctor had on Saturday and Sunday morning, but on Sunday, (yesterday) in the Evening She was suddenly worse. The Doctor Stopp'd all night — this morning, to my inconsolable grief, I found all hopes of recovery was at an end. — I wish I had the means to send for you, I have none. — The Dear Child departed this life in twentyone hours after the last attack, she died in my presence at a little before One O clock this Day, to enjoy everlasting Bliss above, leaving me a Distress'd inconsolable Mortal never more to be happy. The Dreadful Event will shock you too much but I feel bound to relate it to you. My difficulties here are great. My success uncertain for want of a little Money. — My loss is greater in My Dearest Lavinia. She was my only

Stay and Comfort. I can write no more.

Remaining your affectionate and afflicted
husband

William Billingsley.

P.S. I wish you was here but the present uncertain state of my affairs and the want of means — I do not see the prudence or means of attaining that point — and the now troubled state of my mind renders the hope of happiness impossible. The Dear Angel was my prop, my support and comfort in all my troubles since the Death of Her Dear Sister — when Both were living I had their united assistance — think, oh think, — what trouble I have — but all my troubles are to me nothing compar'd with the severe loss of my Dearest Children whom no man ador'd more — My dear Sarah your Grief will be great.

54. Billingsley, William. Letter to his wife. Quoted in E. M. Nance. Batsford, 1942.

NOTE. William Billingsley (Beeley) came to Swansea from the Midlands with his two daughters, seeking an opportunity to use his secret formula for fine china. He was employed at the Cambrian Pottery of the Dillwyns where his elder daughter also worked as a burnisher. She died in Swansea early in 1817 and was buried at St. Mary's. Billingsley had set up a pottery at Nantgarw in 1813 and, on the failure of his Swansea work due to heavy losses in firing, returned there: Lavinia died nine months later.

THOMAS BOWDLER

Yesterday at his residence, the Rhyddings, near Swansea, in the 73rd year of his age, Thomas Bowdler, Esquire, F.R.S. and S.A., editor of the Family Shakespeare and of several valuable and useful publications. In his private habits, Mr Bowdler was zealous and constant in the performance of the great duties of religion and morality — assiduous and inflexible in the pursuit of those who had claims on his charity; in fact, a boundless liberality towards all mankind was the well-known characteristic of this excellent man. His memory will be long revered by a distinguished circle of friends, and his death a lasting resource of regret to the objects of his bounty.

55. The Cambrian. Feb. 1825.

Being unable to obtain an extension of his lease at St. Boniface in the Isle of Wight, or to find another residence in its neighbourhood, Mr. Thomas Bowdler quitted the Isle of Wight in 1810, and in the close of that year with much kindness took upon himself the charge of accompanying his nephew to Malta, and watching his health during the succeeding winter and spring. On his return he fixed his residence at the Rhyddings near Swansea, in a small house situated on rising ground immediately above the sea, and commanding a view of that beautiful bay. The neighbourhood of the sea was to him an object of particular attenion, as it secured to him a mild climate, and the benefit of sea-bathing during some months of the year. Here therefore, during the succeeding years of his life, his winter was spent; and from hence he made excursions to England and Scotland, for the sake of visiting friends and relatives or into foreign parts, either with the same object, or for the benefit of his health.

A literary object of a very different nature, but undertaken with a view to the moral improvement of society, now engaged Mr Thomas Bowdler's attention. This was no less than presenting the plays of Shakespeare to the public, purified from everything that could offend the most delicate eye or ear. Upon this subject two opinions have prevailed in extreme opposition to each other. While some ardent admirers have refused to part with a syllable of his works lest the beauty of the whole should be diminished, others have desired to exclude him from their shelves, lest they who read him should be contaminated. Extremes are generally faulty, and happily in this case a middle course could be adopted with less difficulty than could be imagined till the trial was made; which would leave entire and untouched all that is really valuable, removing only that which is indecent and offensive; which would take away the impurities that have gathered upon the surface, and thereby show to greater advantage the beauty and uniformity of the work. This was attempted some years since by one of Mr Thomas Bowdler's relatives in respect of twenty of the best plays. He himself afterwards carried into execution the same plan with regard to the whole number, and in 1818 published the Family

Shakespeare in ten volumes. 'In which nothing is added to the original text but those words and expressions are omitted, which cannot with propriety be read aloud in a family.

It is certainly my wish, and it has been my study, to exclude from this publication whatever is unfit to be read aloud by a gentleman to a company of ladies.

I can hardly imagine a more pleasing occupation for a winter's evening in the country, than for a father to read one of Shakespeare's plays to his family circle. My object is to enable him to do so without the danger of falling unawares among words and expressions, which are of such a nature as to raise a blush on the cheek of modesty, or to render it necessary for the reader to pause and examine the sequel, before he proceeds further in the entertainments of the evening.'

To those who desire to prohibit the perusual of Shakespeare's plays, arguments of a different kind must be addressed. But in reply to the objections of those, who adopting the opposite extreme are afraid of injuring the dramatist by the slightest mutilation two circumstances may be mentioned; the first is, that the folio edition of 1624 is in many respects much more pure than the earlier editions, and in these respects may be deemed a Family Shakespeare: the second, that in representing the plays of Shakespeare upon the stage, many indecent expressions are always omitted; and without such omission the representation could not be endured. Are these plays now rendered feeble and uninteresting by such mutilations? Or would anyone wish such things to be read in the family, which must not be heard in the theatre? But in fact the question is decided. Seven years have elapsed since the Family Shakespeare was published in 1818; a third edition is now on sale in octavo, and a fourth in duodecimo. The merit of the work therefore, may be considered to be acknowledged and established: the Family Shakespeare will be the edition to lie on the table of every drawingroom; and the name of the editor will be remembered as of one who has perhaps contributed more than any other individual to promote the innocent and rational amusement of well-educated families.

By his will Mr. Thomas Bowdler, mindful of the blessings which he had enjoyed, and the source from which they came, bequeathed £25 to the poor of the parishes of Swansea and

Oystermouth and of Box where he was born.

'I consider these last four bequests as humble marks of gratitude to Almighty God, for the happiness which He has graciously permitted me to enjoy during a considerable portion of my life is the undisturbed tranquillity of these retired, but friendly abodes of peace, and religious, but cheerful meditation.' To the Church of Swansea he also bequeathed a favourite picture by Sasse Ferrati in the following terms: —

> *Whereas I am the possessor of a valuable picture of the Virgin Mary and our Infant Saviour, my wish is that it may be placed, after my death, as an altar piece in the chancel of my parish church of St. Mary, Swansea: thus dedicating this picture to the temple of God, in humble and grateful acknowledgement of the happy tranquillity with which His merciful providence has blessed the evening of my life in the parish; and for this purpose I leave the above mentioned picture in trust.'*

56 Bowdler, Thomas: Memoir of the late John Bowdler, Longman, London, 1825, pp. 298-331.

NOTE. John Bowdler was the father of the Rev. Thomas Bowdler who included a note on his uncle in this biography.

John Bowdler 1746 - 1823) brothers.
Thos. Bowdler 1754 - 1825)
Rev. Thos. Bowdler 1782 - 1856

THOMAS BOWDLER ON MEASURE FOR MEASURE

This comedy contains scenes which are truly worthy of the dramatic poets. Isabella's pleading with Angelo in behalf of mercy to her brother, and afterwards insisting that his life must not be purchased by the sacrifice of chastity, is an object of such interest as to make the reader desirous of overlooking the many great defects which are to be found in other parts of the play. The story is little suited to comedy . . Parts of the play are not without faults. The best characters act too much upon a system of duplicity and falsehood, and the Duke in the first act, trifles cruelly with the feelings of Isabella. Lucio is inconstant and profligate. Lastly the indecent expressions with which many of the scenes abound are so interwoven with the story, that it is extremely difficult to separate the one from the other.

I trust, however, that I have succeeded in doing it, and I should not be sorry if the merit or demerit of the whole work were to be decided by the examination of this very extraordinary play, as it is now printed in the Family Shakespeare.

BOWDLER'S EXCISIONS AND ADDITIONS TO ACT I. SC. 4 OF MEASURE FOR MEASURE

Excisions in Brackets

LUCIO:
Hail, virgin, if you be; as those cheek roses
Proclaim you are no less! Can you so stead me
As bring me to the sight of Isabella,
A novice of this place, and the fair sister
To her unhappy brother Claudio?

ISA:
Why 'her unhappy brother?' let me ask;
The rather for I now must make you know
I am that Isabella and his sister.

LUCIO:
Gentle and fair, your brother kindly greets you.
Not to be weary with you, he's in prison.

ISA:
Woe me! for what?

LUCIO:
(For that, which if myself might be his judge,
He should receive his punishment in thanks:
He hath got his friend with child.)
His friend's with child by him. (inserted by Bowdler).

ISA:
Sir, make me not your story.

LUCIO:
('Tis true
I would not, though 'tis my familiar sin
With maids to seem the lapwing and to jest,
Tongue far from heart, play with all virgins so:)
I hold you as a thing enskied and sainted;
By your renouncement, an immortal spirit;
And to be talked with in sincerity,
As with a saint.

ISA:
You do blaspheme the good, in mocking me.

LUCIO:
Do not believe it. Fewness and truth, 'tis thus:
Your brother and his lover have embraced:
(As those that feed grow full; as blossoming time
That from the seedness the bare fallow brings
To teeming foison, even so her plenteous womb
Expresseth his full tilth and husbandry.

ISA:
Some one with child by him?) My cousin Juliet?

LUCIO:
Is she your cousin?

ISA:
Adoptedly; as school maids change their names,
By vain though apt affection.

LUCIO:
She it is.

ISA:
O, let him marry her!

NOTE. In Act 2 sc 1 the whole scene between Elbow and Froth is cut.

57. Bowdler, Thomas: The Family Shakespeare, Longman Green, 1859. pp. 301-2.

THE TWO PIERS

The machines for bathing are kept half a mile from the town, under the direction of Mrs. Landey, who likewise keeps a lodging house near the place: the charges are twenty-five shillings a week, board and lodging; and ten shillings and sixpence a week for a private parlour.

The harbour of Swansea, which is large, has had great sums expended on it, without much judgement having been evinced in the expenditure: the piers which are extensive, are already frequently wanting considerable repairs, and will always be a source of emolument to those who know how to make the most of a good job.

Swansea is seen to great advantage from the bay, its best front being towards the Channel; it is a mixture of good and bad, of old streets and new, wide and narrow, pride and poverty, much show, and little wealth. The market, which is on Saturday, is greatly improved of late years, and not only affords comforts but luxuries; yet Swansea, except to those who are acquainted with it, is a more expensive place to reside at for a short time than an English watering place: still those lodgings, which are so highly rated during the season, are comfortable retreats to half pay officers during the winter months; and from the mildness of the climate, and many families taking up their residence at it during the period, Swansea, were it not for the faults and greediness or mismanagement of some of its inhabitants, would rise to wealth and respectability.

Its banks are opulent and obliging; and the faculty of that talent and repute, that London houses are left empty, even in winter to have the benefit of Mr Collins' attendance for ladies who are delicate or timid. The playhouse is respectable, and the performers generally good, but badly paid for their exertion. The post office is here very regular and obliging, and conveyances to Bristol, Gloster or London, although expensive, regular and safe. A walk may be comfortably enjoyed in five minutes after a shower, or between showers, without wet feet; and both drives and rides in the vicinity are numerous and beautiful. The libraries are good, well supplied and civil, and the shops accommodating, and plentifully stocked.

58. Cambrian Tourist, 1821.

LAND PORPOISES

Swansea is a large town, containing 13,000 people, carrying on a good trade in iron, copper, brass, tin, coal, lime, culm and earthenware; and possessing an artificial harbour full of vessels. The port is formed by the convergence of two piers running out, one from each side of the mouth of the river. The sea-beach is sandy and smooth; and the breakers that fall on the shore are greatly obstructed in their course, by the numerous land porpoises who flounder in the spray during the bathing season. It is said that Chaucer's great contemporary, Gower, was a child of Swansea; but with what truth we know not now.

A steamer left the harbour while Pedestres stood on the beach; did he yearn for Devonshire as his eye watched her retreat, and diminish to a speck in the offing?

No — poo nonsense — he made a semi-pirouette on his heel, and walked out of the town for the Cromlech.

King Arthur's Cromlech, or as it called, King Arthur's stone, stands on a high and bleak hill about eleven miles from Swansea. This peninsula of land, known by the name of Gower or Gowerland, was peopled by a colony of Flemings, who were washed off the flat soil of their own country by an encroachment of the sea.

We are told that a spring of clear water rises from it, known by the name of Our Lady's Well. This fountain is also said to ebb and flow with the tide of the sea over which it towers to the elevation of some hundred feet: — there was not one drop, however, there at six o'clock P.M. on the 11th of June, 1833. It was all dry when your Pedestres was there. He looked at the sea — the tide was out.

The monument is spoken of in the Triads as one of the great works effected in Britain. Silbury Hill the second, and Stonehenge the third. It is called the stone of Sketty and 'like the work of the Stone of Sketty' has passed into a Welsh proverb to express an undertaking of vast difficulty.

59. Pedestres and Sir Clavileno Woodenpeg: A Pedestrian Tour, Saunders and Otley, 1836, from pp. 346-351.

EDUCATION FOR THE POOR

Swansea, formerly called Abertawe, from its situation near the mouth of the River Tawe, is a seaport town, with upwards of 13,000 inhabitants. It stands near the centre of a beautiful bay of the Bristol Channel, on an angle between two hills, which shelter it from the north-east and north-west winds. The air is mild, and the soil, for a considerable depth gravelly. Some of the streets are modern, wide, and well built; but others are old, narrow and irregular. They are lighted with gas, and the principal have good footpaths.

The Town-Hall, near the south end of the town, is a handsome stone building, erected in 1829. It is approached by two flights of steps, and adorned with columns of the Doric order.

The Castle, situated in the centre of the town, was formerly a building of great extent. The prinicpal part remaining is a massive tower, surmounted by a range of light arches, which support a parapet, in the same style as those at Lamphey Court and St. David's.

Adjoining the Castle is the New Market, built in 1774. The Market-place for corn, fish, and vegetables, is between Wind Street and Castle Street. It is supported by ten pillars of free stone, and the roof is covered with lead from St. David's Cathedral, which Cromwell gave to a gentleman of the town.

Swansea possesses an excellent House of Industry and Infirmary, established in 1817, and situated on the Beach; a free Grammar School founded by Hugh, Bishop of Waterford and Lismore, in the 17c, now kept at Mount Pleasant; as well as Lancasterian and National Schools.

The town has for many years been resorted to as a bathing-place for which the shore is admirably adapted. There are also several warm sea-water and vapour baths, bathing machines, circulating libraries, public rooms, billiard tables, reading rooms, and other attractions for visitors. The inhabitants have, however, the reputation of paying a strict attention to their own interests; and the stranger will find a residence here for a short time quite as expensive as at any other watering place. But during the winter months the lodgings are considerably lower in price and many families then resort thither from other parts of Wales.

The Copper works are also situated on the side of the river, but a mile and a half from the town. The face of the country in their vicinity is literally scorched up by the desolating nature of the copper smoke, which is strongly impregnated with sulphur, arsenic, etc. Notwithstanding, however, the deleterious effects of such an atmosphere, many of the people employed in these works attain a great age.

60. Leigh, Samuel: Guide to South Wales and Monmouthshire, Leigh and Son. London. 1835. pp. 315-6.

THE SOUTH WALES RAILWAY

On the June 18th we were to go down to the opening of the South Wales Railway and accordingly made arrangements to leave London about one. Merthyr had to attend a meeting before starting, so I joined him with the servants at the Paddington Terminus at one. We had a special train for ourselves and some of the Directors, of whom Merthyr is one, and their friends. The speed we went at was wonderful, including many stoppages we reached Bristol in about two hours and a half. At Bristol carriages and four were waiting to convey us forward to Chepstow. When all the party had assembled at the Old Passage we crossed over in the Steamer, and reaching the other side posted on again with all speed to Chepstow. It was glorious summer weather and the journey was most enjoyable. We arrived before seven and found everything prepared for us at the inn.

Next morning we breakfasted at eight and were saluted by ringing bells, and playing of musick and waving flags, etc. We were at the station by nine o clock, and an address having been presented on the auspicous occasion by the inhabitants of the town of Chepstow to the Directors of the Road, we took our places in the carriages, and after some little delay for necessary arrangements, at length set forward on the South Wales railway, amidst all sounds of rejoicing that could be imagined, the firing of cannon and the shouting of the multitude now added to the peals of bells and the bands of music. It was fortunately a glorious day which added greatly to our enjoyment. How lovely Wales is in such weather. Our progress was one of the most triumphant description. At every station we were met and welcomed in the most enthusiastic manner, the Directors having to get out of their carriage at several towns to receive addresses. The shouting, the waving of banners, the excitement of the vast crowds, all full of animation and glee, were most animating, and I fully entered into the spirit of the day, delighted too to be again in my own country, which looks beautiful from the line on every side.

At Cardiff the reception was peculiarly grand, the town having provided a luncheon for the newcomers. The ladies did not leave their carriage but wine was brought to us to drink success to the new undertaking. Thus amid shouts and cheers, through thronging crowds and triumphal arches we made our way to Swansea. By that time our numbers had swelled immensely. The crowd on the platform was very great. The Mayor and Corporation, the Directors and Officials formed in procession at this point and went through the town on foot. The breakfast was given in a tent on the Burrows by the Town of Swansea to the Magnates of the South Wales Road. Six hundred and ninety people sat down to it. But what cared I for the breakfast itself, hungry though I was? The speeches were my delight, and some of them were really good.

61. Guest, Lady Charlotte: Diaries, Murray, pp. 243-4.

NOTE.
Lady Charlotte Guest, 1812-95. born Bertie, only daughter of the 9th earl of Lindsay.
Second wife, married in 1833, of Sir Josiah Guest 1785-1852.
Married Charles Schreiber in 1855.
Welsh scholar, collector of china, fans and playing cards. Benefactor of the South Kensington and British Museums.

Y BREUDDWYD

O na pharasai 'mreuddwyd balmaidd!
Yr oeddwn,tybiais, gyda hi
Ar draeth y môr, a'r awel beraidd
Yn arllwys arnom oddi fry
Aroglau'r gerddi hwnt i'r môr
A'i chwiban llon fel atsain nefol gôr.

Edrychwn arni. O, mor hardd
Y gwrid! Ac O, mor fwyn
Yr olwg daflai ar y bardd —
Ei bardd Islwyn.
'R oedd diniweidrwydd yn ei gwedd
Ac yn ei llygad arlun Hedd.

Gan sangu'n ysgafn, ysgafn, trown i
A chyda gwên ddeallgar, troai hi,
Tuag at y môr, a diolch wnaem ein dau
I'r tonnau.

62. Williams, T. H. Parry: Islwyn, Gwasg Prifysgol Cymru, 1948. pp. 39-40.

NOTE.
William Thomas (Islwyn) 1832-78.
Calvinistic Methodist preacher and poet. Attended Dr. Evan Davies's Academy at Swansea.
Ann Bowen died at 21, just before their marriage, in 1853, and was buried at Crug Las Chapel, Swansea.

GEORGE BORROW IN SWANSEA

Arrived at a place called Glandwr, about two miles from Swansea, I found that I was splashed from top to toe, for the roads were frightfully miry, and was sorry to perecive that my boots were given away at the soles, large pieces of which were sticking out. I must, however, do the poor things justice to say that it was no wonder that they were in this dilapidated condition, for in these boots I had walked at least two hundred miles, over all kinds of paths since I had got them soled at Llangollen. 'Well,' said I to myself,' it won't do to show myself at Swansea in this condition, more especially as I shall go to the best hotel. Seeing a little inn on my right I entered it, and addressing myself to a neat, comfortable landlady, who was standing within the bar, I said —

> *'Please to let me have a glass of ale — and hearkee; as I have been walking along the road, I shall be glad of the services of the 'boots'.'*

'Very good, sir,' said the landlady with a curtsey. Then showing me into a nice little sanded parlour, she brought me a glass of ale, and presently sent in a lad with a boot jack to minister to me. O, what can't a little money effect! For sixpence in that nice small inn I had a glass of ale, my boots cleaned and the excrescences cut off, my clothes wiped with a dwile, and then passed over with a brush, and was myself thanked over and over again.

Starting again with all the spirited confidence of one who has just cast off his slough, I soon found myself in the suburbs of Swansea. As I passed under what appeared to be a railroad bridge, I inquired in Welsh of an ancient-looking man, in coaly habilaments, if it was one. He answered in the same language that it was, then instantly added in English — 'You have taken your last farewell of Wales, sir; it's no use speaking Welsh farther on.'

I passed some immense edifices, probably manufactories, and was soon convinced that, whether I was in Wales or not, I was no longer among the Welsh.

They were taller and bulkier than the Cambrians, and were speaking a dissonant English jargon. The women had much the appearance of Dutch fisher women; some of them were carrying huge loads on their heads. I spoke in Welsh to two or three whom I overtook.

> 'No Welsh, sir.'
> 'Why don't you speak Welsh?' said I.
> 'Because we never learnt it. We are not Welsh.'
> 'Who are you then?'
> 'English; some call us Flamings.'

'Ah, Ah!' I said to myself, 'I had forgot.'

Presently I entered the town, a large bustling, dirty, gloomy place and inquiring for the first hotel was directed to the Mackworth Arms, in Wine St. As soon as I was shown into the parlour

I summoned the 'boots,' and on making his appearance I said in a stern voice: 'My boots want soling; let them be done by tomorrow morning.'

'Can't be, Sir; it's Saturday afternoon; and the shoemaker couldn't begin them tonight.'

'But you must make him!' said I, 'and look here, I shall give him a shilling extra, and you an extra shilling for seeing after him.'

'Yes sir; I'll see after him — they shall be done sir. Bring your slippers instantly. Glad to see you again in Swansea, Sir, looking so well.'

I found the accommodation very good at the Mackworth Arms; and I passed the Saturday evening very agreeably, and slept well throughout the night. The next morning to my great joy I found my boots, capitally repaired, awaiting me before my chamber door. O the mighty effect of a little money!

63. Borrow, George: Wild Wales, Collins, pp. 495-7.

AN EYE FOR COLOUR

This morning we drove to Mumbles, the Westhorps, Miss Brown and myself. As we went through Sketty where Welby was Vicar for 14 years we stopped to look at the Church and Churchyard. The Church is nice but the lychgate is desecrated by the names of all the snobs of Swansea. A tramway runs along the road side from Swansea to Mumbles upon which ply carriages drawn by horses.

Oystermouth Castle stands nobly upon a hill over-looking the town and bay. The lurid copper smoke hung in a dense cloud over Swansea, and the great fleet of oyster boats under the cliff was heaving in the greenest sea I ever saw. We had luncheon upon the Cliffs overlooking the white light-house tower upon the most seaward of the Mumbles.

A shepherd was holloing and driving the sheep of the pasture furiously down a steep place into the sea, and a school of boys came running down the steep green slope, one of them playing 'Rosalie the Prairie Flower' on an accordian as he ran.

A steam tug shot out of Swansea Harbour to meet a heavily

laden schooner under a full press of canvass in the bay and towed her into port, and the great fleet of oyster boats which had been dredging was coming in round the lighthouse point with every shade of white and amber sails gay in the afternoon sun as they ran each into her moorings under the shelter of the great harbour cliff.

As we went along the narrow Cliff path among the gorse towards Langland and Caswell Bay, a flock of strange and beautiful black and white birds flew along the rock faces below us towards the lighthouse piping mournfully. They were I suppose a small kind of gull but they seemed to me like the spirits of the shipwrecked folk seeking and mourning for their bodies. Among the sighing of the gorse came upon the lift of the wind a faint and solemn tolling of a deep bell from seaward. It was the tolling of the buoy bell moored off the Mumbles, a solemn awful sound, for the bell seemed to be tolling for the souls of those who had gone down at sea and warning the living off their graves.

When we came down from the cliff and were going through the town to our inn a furious whirlwind of dust arose and everything was hidden in a dense white cloud. People were obliged to grope for the walls of the houses and cry out to carriages which they could hear but not see not to drive over them!

64. Kilvert, Rev. Francis: Diary, Jonathan Cape, Vol. III. pp. 187-8.

TEMPERANCE IN SWANSEA

Miss Havergal also wrote many small devotional tracts and narratives in prose, all marked by the same earnest and practical piety. Her religious poetry became exceedingly popular in evangelical circles and her hymns are to be found in all collections. Some of her hymns are excellent and will permanently preserve her name.

D.N.B.

From early years she showed exceptional intellectual power but owing to delicate health systematic study was discouraged.

I think it was in April she took (once only) the Y.W.C.A.'s meeting in Swansea for her friend, Miss Morgan. They well remember how she played and sang with them, Precious Saviour, may I live only for Thee! At the close of her address she took round to each a copy of 'Take my life and let it be, etc.' with a blank space that each might sign her name who could do so, in true and loyal allegiance.

The cottagers around us soon won my sister's interest and regard and she invited them to a Bible reading in our house. (I may say that she never began any work of this kind without the Vicar's consent.) My dear sister Frances had promised to meet some men and boys on the village bank on May 21st. Though the day was very damp she went, taking her Bible and her temperance book with her. As she passed thro' the village of Newton, quite a procession gathered round her, her regiment of boys eagerly listening. Her donkey boy Fred Rosser remembers that Miss Frances told him, 'I had better leave the devil's side and get on the safe side: that Jesus Christ's side was the winning side; that He loved us and was calling us and wouldn't I choose Him for my Captain?'

Arriving at home Frances ran in for her book, and on the saddle Fred signed the pledge. A young sailor, W. Hartly was going to sea the next day. Frances was anxious to speak to him and went to the cottage. He signed the book and heard one of her closing messages and this was the last time her feet were 'Swift and beautiful for Thee.'

. . . . . .

Early in October my sister joined me in our Welsh retreat. How I remember her first words to me, 'I wanted so to get to you, Marie dear!' She was so very tired that even the sea air and perfect rest failed to refresh her for some time. Afterwards, she thoroughly enjoyed the walks and scrambles on the cliffs; at low tide springing lightly over boulders to beds of sea-weeds, and rocky pools bright with sea anemones and then calling to me to watch the white-crested waves, 'the wind dashing them back like confirmation veils.' Or watching the vessels with all sails up entering the harbour, she would speak of the abundant entrance into the everlasting kingdom. Delighting in all knowledge she studied the Nautical Almanac and at the top of Mumbles lighthouse learnt all the keeper could tell her. Her tastes were so simple, delighting in wild flowers, and in animals, from the great St. Bernard dogs to pet kittens.

We made her study cosy with home comforts and she called it her workshop. She arranged the pictures; by the door was her motto 'For Jesus' sake only' and her temperance pledge card.

In the South window, its sea view stretching over to Ilfracombe, stood her little table, flowers and easy chair. Her sofa faced the West window with the view of Caswell Bay and its rocks and there the sunsets came which we so often watched together.

Extract from a letter to Miss Tillerton, 28.5.79.

I have got the whole rising generation of the village to sign the pledge (all between eight and sixteen) except two boys who won't sign, three who broke and one girl (going to sign), also about fifty grown-ups. My little lads are splendid: such hearty enthusiasm about it. Temperance meeting tonight, at which I was popularly supposed to be going to speak! but I have to entrust it all to others under God. I dare not let the fact transpire I can't go. They are such affectionate people, these poor Welsh.

65. Havergal, Maria: Frances Ridley Havergal, James Nisbet, 1880 pp. 257, 267, 297.

NOTE.
F. R. Havergal. 1836-1879
Daughter of a writer of sacred music.
Published collections of poems and hymns.
1870: Ministry of Song.
1874: Under the Surface.
1878: Moved to Wales and lived at Caswell Bay Road.
1880: Life Chords.
1883: Life Echoes.
1886: Coming to the King.

A LOCAL NOVELIST:

Besides being a local celebrity Miss Dillwyn also had a claim to national fame for discovering the genius of R. L. Stevenson. Idleness being her one horror, when in her younger days, illness forced her to abandon physical exertion, she took up book reviewing for the Spectator. In 1884 she was given Treasure Island to review, and she led the chorus which acclaimed the author as a genius.

Her dress was masculine except for a serge skirt with two big pockets in which she liked to thrust her hands. She wore a panama or a felt hat according to the season, and she smoked cigars in public.

'I like a smoke, and I can see no objection to it. Let others do what they like: it suits me, and when I do it, I do it openly. I would never consent to smoking in secret.'

She wrote several novels.

66. Western Mail: Obituary Notice, December 14th, 1935.

Do not people's natures, more or less, take after the places where they are born and pass their lives? And is not man much more likely to be rough and wild if he has been brought up in an exposed cottage whose walls rock and shake with every blast of wind, than he would have been if he had lived in some snug valley home, sheltered on all sides by hills and trees and never had any further acquaintance with bad weather, but what I may call an accidental one — that is to say, only knowing about it when he was out of doors — instead of being always in the midst of it, both indoors and out, and compelled to feel and know what it was like wherever he might be?

If I am right in this idea, it will account for the Upper Killay folk being rather a rough set; for Upper Killay stands just at the edge of Fairwood Moor, which is a place where you feel the whole force of every wind that blows, and where there is always some air stirring even though there may be none anywhere else, and where a hailstorm beats against you as if each stone wanted to make a hole through, and come out on the other side.

Properly to understand what the hail there could do, you should have seen the state in which the son of the minister at Three Crosses came home one day, with his face all cuts and bruises and one eye almost closed up.

Upper Killay is so placed that it seems as if its inhabitants must naturally have more or less of a twist towards wildness; and when I was a boy, little or nothing was done to straighten out this natural twist. People did not take so much trouble to improve one another in those days as they do now and it seemed to be taken for granted that the state of life into which a man was born was as unalterable as his colour. If the parents were black, the children would never be white, and if the parents were uncivilized, so would the children be also to the end of their days, and it was no use trying to make them anything else. Ideas have changed since then, and it has become the fashion to be very much interested in the education of the lower classes. There are folk now who make as much fuss about everyone's knowing how to read, and write and spell, and understand poetry, geography, and botany, history and science, and such things, as if there could be neither health, strength nor happiness without all this learning; and schools, churches and chapels are springing up in all directions over the country. But in my time nobody had invented these new ideas, and the chapel at Three Crosses was the only civilising influence as they call it, within reach of Killay. None of the children of the place knew what going to school meant; and, as a rule, we ran wild and amused ourselves by getting into as much mischief as possible from morning to night.

Carriages were a great amusement to us children. Whenever we heard one coming we used to rush out and surround it; some running in front, some at each side, some clinging on behind, and all shrieking and whooping like mad. That is to say, we did this if we were not stopped; but the gentlefolks did not like it, and encouraged their coachmen to cut at us with their whips, so that we got to think that anyone who let us run after his carriage was sure not to be one of the real gentry. The people who suited us best were the Swansea tradespeople, when they went for a day's outing into Gower, and passed through Killay on their way there; for they used to throw us coppers to scramble for, and never minded how much paint we scratched off the vehicle they were in by hanging on to it — as indeed, why should they, when it was a hired one and not their own? We generally liked to run as close as possible to the carriage, so as to look as if we were in danger from it (though in reality we were perfectly safe), for then, if there were any lady who wanted to be thought very feeling, she was sure to begin screaming and hiding her face, and exclaiming, 'Look at the wheel! It will go over the child — it will — I know it will! Oh! how horrid! I can't bear to look! Can't you stop the carriage? Oh! don't let the poor little darling be killed; so send it away!' and such like nonsense, till the favourite young man comforted her, and threw us halfpence to get rid of us.

. . . But with all their fine feelings none of these people ever took the trouble to get out and walk up the long steep Killay hill, so as to lighten the work of the poor animals that had to draw them; nor yet did they seem to see any cruelty in filling a big heavy omnibus as full as it could cram, and making the two half-fed over worked horses drag it and them for some twenty or thirty miles on the hottest days of the year, and go at a trot for the best part of the way, whether it were up hill or down!

67. Dillwyn, E. Amy: Rebecca Rioter, Macmillan, 1880, Vol. I. pp. 5-9.

THE MUMBLES LIFEBOAT

For some days previously the wind had been strong and gusty but about five o-clock it gathered up its strength and blew with great fury and accompanied ever and anon by showers of hail and rain. On the sea coast it expanded all its power and as a result we have to record an awful tale of loss of human life. The first intimation that reached the town was a telegram which was posted up both at the Harbour Office and the Cambrian Office soon after 12.20 p.m. to the effect that a Dantzic barque had gone ashore off the Mumbles Head, losing one of her crew and worse still that in the course of a gallant effort to save life, the Mumbles lifeboat had been stove in and six of her crew had perished.

The lives of two of the lifeboat's crew were saved by Miss Ace, the daughter of the lighthouse keeper who went down to the rocks, up to her waist in water and threw her shawl to the sinking men and so drew them ashore.

68. The Cambrian: Wreck of the Prinz Adalbert, February 2, 1883.

THE WOMEN OF MUMBLES HEAD

Bring novelists, your notebook! bring, dramatists, your pen!
And I'll tell you a simple story of what women do for men.

It's only a tale of a lifeboat, of the dying and the dead,
Of a terrible storm and shipwreck, that happened off Mumbles Head.
Maybe you have travelled in Wales, sir, and know it north and south;
Maybe you are friends with the natives that dwell at Oystermouth;
It happened, no doubt, that from Bristol you've crossed in a casual way
And have sailed your yacht in the summer, in the blue of Swansea Bay.

Well, it isn't like that in the winter, when the lighthouse stands alone,
In the teeth of Atlantic breakers, that foam on its face of stone,
It wasn't like that when the hurricane blew, and the storm bell tolled or when

There was news of a wreck, and the life-boat, and a desperate cry for men.
When in the work did the coxswain shirk? a brave old salt was he!
Proud to the bone of as four strong lads as ever had tasted the sea,
Welshmen all to the lungs and loins, who, about that coast 'twas said,
Had saved some hundred lives a piece — at a shilling or so a head!

It didn't go well with the lifeboat! 'twas a terrible storm that blew,
And it snapped the rope in a second that was flung to the drowning crew;
And then the anchor parted — 'twas a tussle to keep afloat!
But the father stuck to the rudder, and the boys to the brave old boat.

Then at last on the poor doom'd lifeboat a wave broke mountains high!
'God help us now!' said the father, 'it's over my lads goodbye.'
Half of the crew swam shoreward! half to the sheltered caves,
But father and sons were fighting death in the foam of the angry waves.

Up at the lighthouse window two women beheld the storm,
And saw in the boiling breakers a figure — a fighting form,

It might be a grey haired father, then the women held their breath,
It might be a fair haired brother, who was having a round with death;
It might be a lover, a husband whose kisses were on the lips
Of the women whose love is the life of men, going down to the sea in ships:
They had seen the launch of the lifeboat, they had seen the worst and more;
Then kissing each other, these women went down from the lighthouse straight to the shore.

There by the rocks on the breakers these sisters, hand in hand,
Beheld once more that desperate man who struggled to reach the land.
'Twas only aid he wanted to help him across the wave
But what are a couple of women with only a man to save?
What are a couple of women? well more than three craven men
Who stood by the shore with chattering teeth refusing to stir — and then
Off went the women's shawls, sir, in a second they're torn and rent,
Then knotting them into a rope of love, straight into the sea they went!

'Come back!' cried the lighthouse keeper, 'For God's sake, girls, come back!'
As they caught the waves on their foreheads, resisting the fierce attack.
'Come back!' moaned the greyhaired mother, as she stood by the angry sea,
'If the waves take you, my darlings, there's nobody left to me.'
'Come back!' said the three strong soldiers, who still stood faint and pale,
'You'll drown in the face of the breakers! You will fall if you brave the gale!'

'Come back!' said the girls,' we will not! go tell it to all the town
We'll lose our lives, God willing, before that man shall drown.'

'Give one more knot to the shawls, Bess! Give one strong clutch

of your hand!
Just follow me, brave, to the shingle, and we'll bring him safe to land!
Wait for the next wave, darling, only a minute more,
And I'll have him safe in my arms, dear, and we'll drag him safe to the shore.'
Up to the arms in water, fighting it breast to breast,
They caught and saved a brother alive! God bless us we know the rest —
Well many a heart beats stronger, and many a tear was shed,
And many a glass was tossed right off to the Women of Mumbles Head.

69. Scott, Clement: The Women of Mumbles Head, Samuel French, 1883.

WHERE OUGHT THE WELSH UNIVERSITY TO BE?

THE CLAIMS OF MERTHYR

It being now settled that Wales is to be placed on a par in educational advantage with England, Scotland, and Ireland, by having a University of her own, the time has arrived when it is fitting and even necessary that the claims of the various towns of Wales for the location of the two colleges should be laid before the public. The object of this paper, however, will not be to depreciate other towns, but to urge the claims of Merthyr Tydvil as a town admirably suited for the erection of the proposed University of Wales. It might be urged with considerable force that, as Merthyr is known far and near to be Metropolis of Wales, it would be unfair to ignore the claims of a town for scholastic purposes which has so largely contributed by its commercial industries to make Wales famous among the civilised countries of the world..

Williams, R. Nestor.

THE CLAIM OF SWANSEA

If a false step be taken, and the college be misplaced, much of the good it will do might be lost, and possibly another failure may have to be recorded. Nothing is more likely to lead to this result than to be led astray by a phrase, the claim of this place or that, whose inhabitants may wish, or whose authorities may agitate for the honour of being the collegiate town.

Swansea is the centre of the population. It is also the geographical centre — the point of convergence or centre of the Railway System of South Wales. That Swansea is the most accessible point for persons from all parts of the six counties must be taken to be acknowledged, by the fact that it has been chosen for the Assizes or Gaol deliveries held twice a year for all those counties.

The only way in which a pretence that Cardiff is a convenient centre can be manipulated is by taking on to Wales a part of England, the County of Monmouth. To build a college for the Welsh at Cardiff would be so to place it that it would be more convenient for Gloucestershire than for two thirds of those for whom owing to their exceptional poverty and peculiar circumstances it is to be provided.

Nor will Swansea yield the palm, without a protest, to any rival in any other respects. Cut off by a line of hills from Landore and its works, situated on a southern slope of gorse-crowned hills, stretching down to the shore — not a distant mud-bank, but a sandy beach, over which the tide rushes to her very feet — Swansea looks out on a bay not easily surpassed in beauty and is swept by the breeze, unsullied by the breath of man, fresh from the Atlantic.

Glascodine, Charles Henry:

NOTE.
The University College of Swansea was founded in 1920.

THE CLAIMS OF CARDIFF

I do not believe that the choice will fall on Swansea, as in my opinion when weighed in the balance with Cardiff it will be found wanting in the main points upon which its claims must be based.

FIRST. Is Cardiff central in situation? By central I do not mean geographically and geometrically in the middle of an area of country but as near as possible in the heart of the population. I am of the opinion that the districts of Carmarthen and that part of South Wales which lies west of Carmarthen may, and ought to be excised, as Aberystwyth would not only be the most easy of access, but would require their support.

SECOND. Does Cardiff possess a large and increasing population of varied industries, with facilities of access and a reputation for health?

THIRD. Are the social status and requirements of the population such as would justify the supposition that from it could be drawn a larger proportion of students than from any other available district of corresponding areas?

It is not necessary that I should further discuss my subject.

Williams, Lewis:

The University College of Cardiff was established in 1883.

70. The Red Dragon: Vol. I. Feb. — July, 1882, p. 84.

THE BRITISH ASSOCIATION IN SWANSEA

When the district of Gower came to be dealt with the editor found little or nothing to edit, for which reason so much of this book as relates to that subject has involved much original labour. That it should have been left for one whose connection with west Glamorgan is not hereditary but adoptive to supply the deficiency, is, at least, a matter for comment; but until a native topographer, — a new Giraldus, — steps forward to record worthily the beauties of his own coast and valleys, this book claims, more adequately than any other to do so.

> Linger with me this olden land to spy: —
> A land of sleepy hollows, hemmed with woods
> And hill slopes dense with deep-roof'd solitudes;
> Of wind-racked moors oe'r which the curlews cry,
> And the red waves of rolling gorse-fires fly:
> Of capes and scaurs, sea-hewn in stormiest moods,
> And roaring caves, that nurse the kestrel broods,
> Where once old-world carnivora crawled to die.

A land whereon the breath of Arthur's praise
Floats like mist; around whose rock-bound coast
Lie Philip's galleons rooted fast in sand, —
Hovers in storm time many a drowned ghost;
A shore for song a land of yesterdays,
Linger with me about this haunted land.

71. Woods, James Chapman: British Association Guide to Swansea. (Ed:) 1883.

TO M.W.

From the dun heath where sounds the plover,
From moonlit pastures starred with dew,
Long since my heart has flown to cover
With you.

Now, though life lifts a warning finger
And climbing shadows dusk the blue,
Yet here my heart is fain to linger
With you.

So may Death find us fast abiding
In faith as deep, in love as true,
As when my heart went first in hiding
With you.

72. Woods, James Chapman: A Pageant of Poets, 1931.

Mr Woods is skilled and melodious, if rather a mournful singer. Genuine inspiration is his, a rare mastery of forms of metre, and a felicity of expression that seldom fails him. His book is one of great intrinsic merit and charm and of still higher promise for the future.

The Scotsman: Review of Child of the People, by James Chapman Woods.

A Pageant of Poets shows him in all his mature logic and scholarship: it shows the critical mind at its best, but it is not

Royal Institution & Countess of Huntingdon's Chapel 1852

Guildhall 1847

Landore Viaduct 1841

The Terminus, Swansea 1841

Mumbles Lighthouse

Oystermouth

The Market

National School 1852

Craig-Y-Nos 1905

Singleton Abbey

CASTLE STREET, FEBRUARY, 1941 ALFRED JANES
[MRS. JOHN EVANS]

SELF PORTRAIT, c. 1932 ALFRED JANES

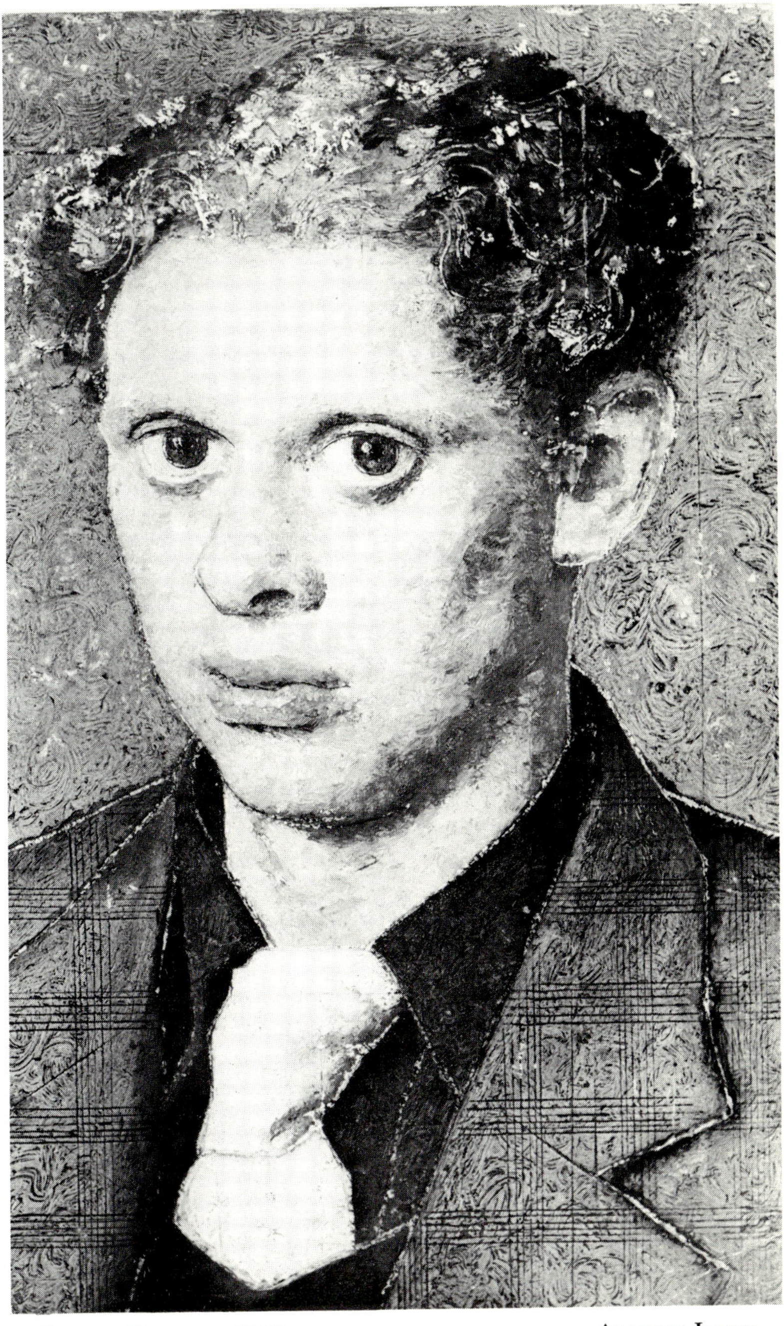

Dylan Thomas, 1934 — Alfred Janes

[National Museum of Wales]

VERNON WATKINS, 1948 ALFRED JANES
[GLYNN VIVIAN ART GALLERY]

what a reader of A Child of the People would expect. It is Mr Wood's most accomplished volume. There they pass, Landor, Southey, Coleridge, Wordsworth, Scott, Byron, Shelley, Keats, and that dignified old commentator, James Chapman Woods.

That is, surely, a fit destiny for him, to be linked, though he has no call to greatness, along with the great, a man who has appreciated, valued, and mirrored what the undying have said.

73. Thomas, Dylan: James Chapman Woods, in Herald of Wales, April 23, 1932. sub-title—Swansea's greatest poet.

Youth calls to age across the tired years:
'What have you found,' he cries, 'what have you sought?'
'What you have found,' age answers through his tears,
'What you have sought.'

74. Note. Quoted from a poem accompanying the above article, entitled Youth calls to age.

DANIEL WOODROFFE (MRS WOODS)

With a feeling of utter consternation he looked out into the corridor. Asta's door was open — A sense of coming misfortune was weighing him down. Yes, Asta's door was open; the room had a dismantled air. Skene stood within the door in the glaring sunlight. His face was pallid; his figure looked thin; he was watching a steamer which was crossing in the direction of Trouville.

Trouville lay over there to the left — a little, indistinct cloud on the horizon; but tonight it would be gay and glittering and the light of his poor lost love would flame like a falling star above the sea line.

75. Woods, Mrs. James Chapman (Daniel Woodroffe): Tangled Trinities, Heinemann, 1901, pp. 276, 280.

Note. Other novels:— The Beauty Shop
The Evil Eye
Her Celestial Husband.

A TRANSATLANTIC VIEW

Welsh amusements are on the whole a very good indication of

the moral tone of Welsh minds. And these, as is well known, are mainly of an innocent or musical character — lectures, concerts, eisteddfodau. It is unnecessary to enlarge on the Eisteddfod. A Welsh concert will often prove to be a far more impressive and character-suggestive thing than a mere entertainment furnished forth by hired singers and instrumentalists. It not infrequently happens that the whole audience will break out in chorus, singing in a way to make the rafters hum. And fancy what such a chorus may chance to be when it is possible the audience may be numbered in thousands, and every man, woman and child is able to sing . . .

In Aberdare, one Christmas, nearly four thousand persons paid for admission to hear the Oratorio of Samson in the old hall whence Caradoc's famous musical squadron marched on London; and I was assured that nine tenths of this vast audience were Welsh working men, with their wives and sweethearts and they could all sing, too, after a fashion.

The theatre fills a very small place in the life of Welsh towns. There are but four towns in Wales which have any place they call a theatre — Cardiff, Swansea, Newport and Brecon — all in South Wales, it will be noticed.

Nevertheless, the Christmas pantomime on Boxing Night is well patronised. The theatres are packed on this night if on no other of the year, to witness the delights of Jack and Jill or The Pretty Prince.

There is a marked catering in the doggerel of the first part, to the tastes of the working classes. This is natural, as the house is filled with workingmen and servants. They occupy not only the gallery and the pit — for the pit is an institution which still holds its own in Welsh theatres, precisely as it did fifty years ago — but they also fill the boxes and the dress circle. The dress circle is rather a misnomer. Generally it is empty, or has a few young men about town lounging it in lordly fashion. On a Boxing Night it is occupied but not by very dressy people. The pit takes up the space which in London Theatres is sacred to the orchestra stalls — i.e., the best seats in the house. In London theatres there is a sort of pit but it is behind the velvet field of the luxurious orchestra stalls — at the back of the theatre, under the overhanging balcony, and almost in darkness. The Welsh pit is more primitive and its presence is one great bar to the prosperity of the drama in Wales, for society can hardly be expected to greatly favour an institution which carefully gives up the best places to those who are not in society.

At present it might almost be said that the theatre fills no place at all in the life of the better classes. Society knows it not: the vast majority of religious taboo it; its regular patrons are the lower orders. There are, of course, individuals who form an exception to the rule, who, while belonging to society or to the church, still have a taste for this sort of amusement, and seek to gratify it occasionally and there are exceptional stars or musical organisations to which society does from time to time pay attention. But it may safely be said that the drama will never flourish until the pit, that relic of a past age, is moved out of sight of the fastidious.

A full dress concert is indeed the highest public expression of the upper ten's existence that is seen outside the churches. Usually it is on behalf of some charity or some military organisation, and is patronised quite as much on that account as because of the merit of the performance.

76. Sikes, Wirt: Old South Wales, Sampson Low, 1881, pp. 272-4.

NOTE. Of U.S. Consulate, Cardiff.

THE GOWER INN

October had come and the greatest summer within my memory had broken up. Swansea which is hard by Neath at the mouth of the next valley, that same romantic Tawe, looked at its very worst; and Swansea, though even more finely placed by nature than Neath, is quite the most untoward-looking town in South Wales. Whether the smelting of copper is especially conducive to a dismal aspect I know not, but Swansea to the unaccustomed even is doleful beyond words. Its well-to-do folk perched upon the mountain slopes around find infinite compensation up there, no doubt, for the hours expended in the murky hive below, which is said, moreover, to contain not a single first class street. I have threaded its highways on two or three occasions, though in hasty and uncritical fashion, I admit, but I should be inclined to think that this taunt of its neighbours was not libellous. However that may be, it is much better to be dirty and busy than ornamental and working half-time, and Swansea appeared to be working full blast.

Now Swansea is actually in Gower, and is a leading illustration of what prodigious contrasts within a narrow compass this little island of ours can show. Port Eynon is also in Gower — very much so, indeed — being almost at the extreme point of the peninsula. It is seventeen miles away, and Swansea is its nearest market town and virtually its nearest station. Now Port Eynon is at the end of the world, and almost suggestive of Aberdaron at the point of Lleyn in its astonishing seclusion. But Port Eynon has a bus that thrice a week makes the laborious journey to and from its metropolis. I had contracted some acquaintance in remoter Wales with the nature of these indispensible but archaic survivals; so consigning my traps only to its care, I mounted a bicycle, and pursuing the now rain-soaked highway through the straggling and leafy suburbs of Swansea, and climbing up the long hill through Sketty, I found myself in three or four miles clear of every trace of urban life, and looking out from an expanse of breezy moorland over most of Gower and much of South Wales.

Gower is nearly twenty miles long by five or six miles in width, and has over fifty miles of sea coast, mainly rugged and often magnificent of aspect. Like Pembroke, it has nurtured two distinct races side by side for seven or eight hundred years. But the greater part of the peninsula is English; the smaller is Welsh, and lies on the north-eastern slope facing Carmarthenshire. The line between them, geographically and socially, is almost as sharp as that in Pembroke. It used to be said that when an English Gowerian was asked for the house of a Welsh neighbour just over the line, he generally replied; 'I donna knaw, a lives somewhere in the Welsherie.'

But the Gower man outside the Welsherie is no more Welsh than a Devonian, though he is not like a Devonian. His vices and virtues are entirely his own, and his language, like that of South Pembrokeshire, is an English vernacular evolved in isolation. To use a convenient term, his stock, his character and speech are Teutonic. The attitude of the Gower rustic when you touch on the matter in conversation with him is not devoid of humour. It is enough for him, of course, that he is a Gower man and not a Welshman, though he does not seem to repudiate the Cymric affinity with the same fervour of pride and prejudice that a Pembrokeshire man would. The community is of course a much smaller one, and he takes his racial aloofness merely as a fact, not as a happy dispensation of Providence as well. 'We donna knaw exactly what we are sir; some of the gentry says we're Flemings.' is a stock reply, but there is beyond doubt some sort of satisfaction in belonging to this compact community of far back colonists, and even a little pride in that very mystery which excites such interest 'among the gentry.' but with all their broad Teutonic speech there seemed to me an unmistakeable touch of the Welsh lilt not noticeable in Pembrokeshire, and here and there a suggestively Anglo-Welsh word, such as 'iss, iss' (for yes, yes'). Till quite recently there was an old court in Swansea held twice a year, known as the court of Gower Anglicana, where the English of Gower did suit and service and another for the Welsh, known as the Court of Gower Wallica.

Gower was not included in the old lordship of Glamorgan, which stretched from the Rhymney to the Tawe, but was thrown into Glamorganshire, when the new county was formed by Henry VIII. The meaning of Gower or Gwyr has defied interpretation, and exasperated generations of philologists. It was conquered independently soon after Fitzhamon's seizure of Glamorgan, the Norman undertaker in this business being Henry de Newburgh, Earl of Warwick, and it is said to have taken him eight years to drive the Welsh off the peninsula and make himself reasonably secure on it by a sufficient number of castles. Soon afterwards came those batches of Flemings dispatched to South Wales by Henry I. Flooded out of their own country, as tradition has it, they sought fresh territory of the English king, who, by dumping them down here, got rid of them in a graceful way, and at the same time procured a useful and permanent garrison for his own buccaneering barons.

The interior of Gower contains a delightful variety of scene: high ridges of heathery moorland, snug seats embosomed in fine timber, bosky glens through which bright trout streams prattle and sea-coast of every imaginable kind embellished not seldom by the presence of some imposing relic of border strife. There are ancient little churches too, characteristic of a peculiar people and an isolated alien community; and always close at hand are vantage points whence you may look out over wide waters to the rugged capes of Pembroke, to the bounds of Cornwall, the hills of Devon and Somerset, and to the lofty mountains of Brecon. Yet no one penetrates into further Gower save a few enlightened natives of the adjoining coast towns, who spend quiet holidays in the simple accommodation of its primitive seacoast hamlets.

It is a breezy common above Sketty, a couple of miles or so of open fern and heather, over which the road goes trailing westward, that makes one first conscious of being actually in Gower, and of having shaken off the last trace of Swansea's remotest suburbs. Peewits and starlings, in quite remarkable numbers and of surprising friendliness, had the waste to themselves as I traversed it, and dropped down the long slope into the pretty dingle of Park Mill, where, together with a few other cottages, stands the Gower Inn. It was erected by Mr. Penrice of Killvrough (in the last century) an old country seat above, whose woodlands contribute liberally to the arcadian charm for which the spot has some local reputation. A kindly thought for tourists or potential tourists seems to have been the motive of this former squire, for then there was no inn where any but the hardiest wayfarer might lay his head.

77. Bradley, A. G.: In the March and Borderland of Wales. 1905.

AN EARLY ATTEMPT AT IMPROVING SWANSEA, 1895

THE PLANTING OF THE TREES

As I ponder o'er the wordy
Budgets of the local news —
Chronicles that oft offend one
But as frequently amuse —

I have read of naught that gentle
Beauty-loving arts will please
More, with promise of the future
Than, the planting of the trees.

Nature gave her richest dowry
To bedeck fair Swansea's sight,
Verdant hills for view and shelter
Groves for shadow and delight.

And a pure translucent river
Flowing 'twixt the fertile lands
To a Bay, whose playful waters
Dance upon the yellow sands.

O'er that scene of native beauty
Man has passed as with a scourge
Changing oaks and elms to chimneys
For the furnace and the forge.

Making all the verdant valley —
As if by a demon's spite —
With gigantic Shapes and Shadows
The inferno of the Night.

Mid the shrieking of his engines
In the smoke himself hath made
Man hath immolated Nature
To the modern God of Trade.

Everything that's worth achieving
Must be won by slow degrees
Swansea makes a good beginning
By 'the planting of the trees.'

78. Gamwell, S. C.: Poems, Cambrian Office, 1897, p. 21.

NOTE.
S. C. Gamwell, of Hafod.
Apprenticed to E. & J. Griffiths, printers.
Taught French, Latin and shorthand by Professor Benvenuti.
At 20, reporter for the Cambrian; later, for the Herald.
Joint editor, then editor.
'The Cleverest pressman in South Wales.'
Wrote under name of Pierre Claire. (His second name was Clearstone).
"When trees were first planted in Swansea streets, he regarded their introduction as the beginning of a new era in the art of the town." The Cambrian: Obituary, Dec. 18, 1896.

PATTI IN HER WELSH MOUNTAIN HOME

by S. G. Gamwell

Ye wild winds that wander o'er Brecon's high mountains
With musical message, like minstrels of old,
Attuning your harps to the drip of the fountains,
And chanting the anthems of Nature — behold!

There slumbers tonight in your valley's dark portals —
(Ah hush! Ye might wreck her repose with your song)
A being who ranks with the mighty immortals
But whose gifts for a while to this planet belong.

It is Patti! — the Light and the Life of the nations,
The Genius of Music, the Goddess of Art,
The Cantatrice crowned by the world's acclamation
As Queen, nay as Empress of Ear and of Heart.

She has stolen away from the clamour of cities,
Awhile in the Temple of Nature to rest,
As the nightingale weary of warbling her ditties
Lays down her sweet head in the shade of the nest.

Sleep, Wanderer, sleep — Here no envy can harm thee;
Here the murmurs of Mischief and malice shall cease
No troublesome fancies of fears need alarm thee
In this rustic retreat of contentment and peace.

Tall sentinel Hills, that keep guard o'er the valley,
With shadows benignant bend over her close,
Let no spirits unclean or inimical rally
To disturb the fair sleeper 'neath dark Craig-y-nos.

But in murmurous whispers, ye winds and ye waters
With lullaby lays her sweet dreamings invade,
As the lovers of Italy's beautiful daughters
Enliven the night with their soft serenade.

And at morn, when the sun, thro' the foliage peering
Shoots into the vale his gold arrows of light,
Let the chorus of birds hail her welcome appearing
And their madrigals fill all the day with delight.

Thus Diva, if Nature to know thee were able
At the gracious approach all the landscape would start
As when Orpheus fingered his lute in the fable
All Creation acknowledged the spell of his Art.

81. Ibid. 79.

NOTE.
Adelina Juana Maria Patti 1843-1919.
Born in Paris. Settled with parents in America.
First appearance in Lucia di Lammermoor.
Last Appearance, for the Red Cross, October 1914, aged 72, at Royal Albert Hall, London.

PANYGEYRIC ON SWANSEA

How wicked it was of you, dear Mrs. Linton,
To write such deliciously flattering things!
Would you have us believe that the County of Swansea
Is peopled by angels with white feather wings?
Your vision is keen, but your heart is so kindly
That surely it carries you — sometimes — astray.
Your words are as sweet as the sweetness of honey
And welcome to Swansea as hawthorne in May;
But P.C.
Fears that he
With some of your sentiments dare not agree.

You tell us our townfolk are courteous as clever,
And able on all sorts of themes to converse,
In languages many with nous and with clearness —
Theology, politics, hist'ry and verse.
In fact, you have drawn so entrancing a picture
In colours as bright as your own high renown
That some of us, blinded by sudden surprisal
In hourly bewilderment walk through the town;

And P.C.
Marvels how he
And others have failed all these merits to see.

79. S. C. Gamwell (Pierre Claire): On Mrs. E. Lynn Linton's Panygeyric on Swansea; in 'Poems.'

A WILLING EXILE

Baroness Cederstrom, better known to Swansea people perhaps as Madame Patti, this afternoon paid a visit to see the wounded soldiers who arrived there yesterday. The great diva's sympathy for the gallant little nation is intense, and in order to express it more fully she has consented tc emerge from her retirement and sing at a concert in London on Saturday next organised on behalf of the Belgian Relief Fund. The Baroness motored from Craig y nos Castle, and reached the hospital shortly after three o'clock where the staff and secretary, Mr. W. D. Hughes, made the necessary arrangements.

Baron Cederstrom, who is lying at a Swansea nursing home is making good progress.

80. Cambria Daily Leader: October 20, 1914.

SUPERTRAMP IN SWANSEA

The following morning I was up and on my way before the downrighter had put in an appearance. In two or three days I was again back on the outskirts of London, walking it round in a circle.: sometimes ten miles from its mighty heart, or as far distant as twenty miles; but without courage to approach nearer, or to break away from it altogether.

Whatever luck I had, good or bad, I always managed to escape the workhouse; and was determined to walk all night, if needs be, rather than seek refuge in one of those places. One desperate hour possessed me every day, sometimes in the morning, but more often in the evening, when I would way lay people on the high roads, go boldly to front doors of houses, interview men in their gardens, stables or shops, at the same time flourishing before their eyes a whip of a dozen laces. In this hour I seemed to be impelled by a fatality like that of the Wandering Jew, cursed at having to perform something against my will. When this mad fit was at an end, during which I generally succeeded in getting a shilling or more, people might come and go without fear of being molested, for I was satisfied that the workhouse was defeated for another night.

One morning at the beginning of December, I made up my mind to tramp home for Christmas. This was a new idea, and not much to my liking, for I had always written hopeful letters, and although they knew that I had left London, they knew nothing of my present condition. As usual, under these active impulses I made astonishing progress, being on the borders of Wales in less than a week. The greater part of the journey accomplished, being less than thirty miles away from my native town, I regretted having started with such an intention, and tramped over the Welsh hills, day after day, ultimately finding my way to Swansea. I did not remain long in that town, but began other rambles, and the day before Christmas Eve was in a town twenty seven miles from home. Keeping up a pace of three miles an hour in spite of the leg and the rough, uneven roads of the hills, I accomplished the journey in nine hours, arriving home just after dark without having rested on the way.

I had now been tramping for over three months and thought myself entitled to a rest, if such could be had. After all, why had I done this, and to what end had I suffered? For I would now draw the few pounds that were due to me, would return to London in a week or two, and would commence writing without any prospect of success, for I would once more be living on a small income. And such was the case: three weeks' comfort improved me wonderfully and vitality returned stronger than ever, after the low state into which I had fallen. What cut me to the heart was not so much that I had not practised writing during these four months, but that I had been forced to neglect reading and had therefore been taking in no means to justify my hopes in the future of being capable of writing something of my own. The poor man who has his daily duties to perform, has his quiet evenings at home, with friends to lend him books and being known in the locality, a library from which to borrow them, but what privilege has the wanderer?

Feeling myself fit, I drew what money was due to me and returned to London.

82. Davies, W. H.: Autobiography of a Supertramp, Jonathan Cape, 1908, pp. 228-9.

NOTE.
W. H. Davies 1871-1940
Born at Pillgwenlly, Newport.
Son of an iron-moulder.
Apprenticed as a carver and gilder.
Lost a foot in a train accident in Canada in 1899.
First book published in 1905.
'At his best his work compares favourably with the finest lyrics of the English language.' D.W.B.

THE DIRTY WITCH

I have seldom received a fiercer shock than when, from a few lines of appreciation, as beautiful as sympathetic, in this morning's Roll of Honour in the Times I learned that Edward Thomas had given his life in this war. It was the life of one who knew and loved England, its inhabitants and writers, old and new, better than any man I ever came across. Thomas had what are vaguely called Celtic characteristics; he was, as his name betokens, Welsh, and he sorrowed at times over the loss of his birthright in the Cambrian tongue. He knew Wales and its taverns intimately from the Worm's Head to Penmaenmawr. (I met him once in the Gower Inn and once on the summit of Carreg Cennyn Castle.) 'Wild Wales' he savoured intensely and I expect he knew nearly as much Welsh as Borrow.

83. Seccombe, Thomas: Foreword to The Last Sheaf.

A great many people know that Swansea is a Welsh seaport and a manufacturing town — but this I cannot understand: that some people should be — and some are — indifferent to Swansea.

Year after year I go there (I do not mean to Mumbles, but the town, and nothing but the town), and walk up and down it and round about, inhaling sea and mountain air, or the smells from copper works, cobalt works, manure works, and fried fish shops; year after I have felt that only friends could bring me again to Swansea. But the town is a dirty witch. You must hate or love her, and I both love and hate her, and return to her as often as four times in a year. It is not this or that beautiful or hideous thing that draws me. I do not go to see a woman pitching broken crockery out of her front door into a street where children go barefooted; nor to smell the stale fat of the skinyard, and see the shaggy cattle driven into the slaughter house, and a woman carrying a baby in a shawl after them; nor to hear midnight quarreling in the Irish quarter — a woman at first having it her own way, shouting louder and louder and drowning the man's bass interjections, then wildly screaming, Bastard, bastard, until the cry is smothered in noises of scuffling and throttling, and the victor's voice rising for a moment as he strikes, and, after that, her sobbing and moaning that ends in silence broken only by the child they have awakened.

The pleasing accidents are many in Swansea. The docks are always pleasant with the smell of tar, the weaving whirl of the sea-gulls, the still ships, the cool green water reflecting the gaudy figure-head of the Kate, the man unloading potatoes, the painter slung under the bowsprit, with a fag in his mouth, which he puts behind his ear to whistle 'Away to Rio.'

I like, too, the rag-and-bone man blowing one deep note on his horn as he travels mean streets; and the cockle women (their white scoured cockle tubs on their heads or under their arms) from Penclawdd, dressed in half a dozen thicknesses of flannel, striped and checked, all different and all showy — with broad hips, no waists, stout legs slowly and powerfully moving — and the clearest of complexions and brightest of lips and eyes under their soft brown hair.

These pleasant and unpleasant things, however, have little to do with the final effect, composite but very definite of the whole town: they colour certain days but no more. What counts most is the careless, graceless nature of Swansea, its lovely assemblage of chimney-stacks, its position at a river mouth between mountains and the neighbourhood of the sea. Cheapness, Clapham-junction squalor or actual hideousness is everywhere in contrast with grandeur and even sublimity.

The low waterside crowd of copper, steel, tin, zinc or silver, cobalt and manure works is the real Swansea. The remainder, the miles of flat-faced cottages here or there upon the hill, is but an inexpensive prison where the workers may feed, smoke, read the newspapers, breed and sleep. Those works vomit smoke which Swansea people either ignore or praise: for when the smell of the manure works pervades the town, they expect fine weather from a north or north-east wind. They take you up on Townhill at night to see the furnaces in the pit of the town blazing scarlet, and the parallel crossing lines of lamps, which seem, like the stars, to be decoration. If it is always a city of dreadful day, it is for the moment at that distance a city of wondrous night.

By day the scene is better because the variety is greater and because then can be seen the dim ridges of the greater mountains beyond the chimneys and in the other direction a hundred moods of the sea and the coast hills. The furnaces, the fuming slag hills, the grouped or single chimneys standing irregularly beside the river are more worth looking at than a model town. As for the chimneys, like gigantic tree trunks or temple pillars that have survived some gigantic desolation, these and their plumes of smoke or of flame are among the most unforgettable things that men have made. The black hills and vales of Landore, its fire palaces and hundred smoke stacks compose one of the sublimest of all absolutely human landscapes.

At present Swansea is probably more a village than when the borough counted about a thousand under Elizabeth, its activity in spreading hither and thither has kept it from thinking about anything but factories, docks, and the necessities of life. That is the dark charm of Swansea to one who has not to live in it. It is careless of itself, of its majestic position, its lovely neighbourhood, its 120,000 men, women and children. Compared with Cardiff it is a slattern. Yet I am glad to have known Swansea between these hills. Equally shameless and unpretentious, it swarms about the Tawe, climbs over the hills with inconsiderate vitality, always allowing the magnitude and precipitousness of its hills to have full effect, while they, in their turn emphasise the rustic squalor and confused simplicity of the town, combining with it to make a character which at the same time irritates and fascinates.

84. Thomas, Philip Edward: The Last Sheaf, Jonathan Cape, 1928, pp. 151-6.

P. E. Thomas 1879-1917
Born in Lambeth: father in the Civil Service.
St. Paul's and Lincoln College, Oxford.
Lived by reviewing and writing commissioned books.
Enlisted in July, 1915: killed at Arras in 1917.
Wrote poems under the name of Edward Eastway.
1920 Collected Poems.

D.W.B.

PREMONITION 1936

The fact that we set fire to the buildings and building materials at the Penrhos Range is not in dispute. We ourselves were the first to give the Authorities warning of the fire, and we proclaimed to them our responsibility. Yet we hold the conviction that our action was in no wise criminal, and that the responsibility for any loss due to our act is the responsibility of the English government.

We are professional men who hold positions of trust, of honour, and of security. I must speak now with reluctance for myself. I profess the literature of Wales in the University College of Wales in Swansea. That is my professional duty. It is also my pride and my delight. Welsh literature is one of the great literatures of Europe. It is the direct heir in the British Isles of the literary discipline of classical Greece and Rome. And it is a living, growing literature, and draws its sustenance from a living language and a traditional social life. It was my sense of the inestimable value of this tremendous heirloom of the Welsh nation that first led me from purely literary work to public affairs, and to the establishment of the Welsh National Party. It was the terrible knowledge that the English Government's Bombing Range, once it were established in Lleyn, would endanger and in all likelihood destroy an essential focus of this Welsh culture, that made me think my own career, the security of my family, things that must be sacrificed in order to prevent so appalling a calamity. From the University lecture rooms I have not professed a dead literature of antiquarian interest. I have professed the living literature of this nation. So that this literature has claims on me as a man as well as a teacher. I hold that my action at Penrhos aerodrome on September 8th saves the honour of the University of Wales, for the language and literature of Wales are the very raison d'ètre of this University . . .

Everywhere in Europe today we see Governments asserting that they are above the moral law of God; that they recognise no other power but the power of the State. These governments claim absolute powers; they deny the rights of persons and of moral Persons. They deny that they can be challenged by any code of morals, and they demand the absolute obedience of men. Now that is atheism. It is the denial of God, of God's Law. It is the repudiation of the entire Christian tradition of Europe, and it is the beginning of the reign of chaos.

We deny the absolute power of the State-God. Here in Wales, a land that has no tradition except Christian tradition, a land that has never in all its history been pagan or atheist, we stand for the preservation of that Christian tradition and for the supremacy of the moral law over the materialistic bureaucracy.

We hold with unshakeable conviction that the burning of the monstrous Bombing Range in Llyn was an act forced on us for the defence of Welsh civilisation, for the defence of Christian principles, for the maintenance of the Law of God in Wales.

We ask you to be fearless. We ask you to bring in a verdict that will restore Christian principles in the realm of law, and open a new period in the history of nations and governments. We ask you to say we are not guilty.

85. Lewis, J. Saunders and Valentine Lewis: 'Why we burnt the Bombing School, Swyddfa'r Blaid, Caernarfon, pp. 4, 8, 18.

OLD SWANSEA'S FUNERAL PYRE

The burnt-out clock of St. Mary's has come to a stop,
And the hand still points to the figure that beckons the
house-stoned dead.
Child Shades of my ignorant darkness, I mourn that
moment alive
Near the glow-lamped Eumenides' house,*1* overlooking the
ships in flight,
Where Pearl White focussed our childhood, near the foot of
Cwmdonkin Drive,

To a figment of crime stampeding in the posters' wind-blown
blight.

I regret the Broken Past, its prompt and punctilious cares,
All the villanies of the fire-and brimstone-visited town.
I miss the painter[2] of limbo at the top of the fragrant stairs,
The extravagant hero[3] of night, his iconoclastic frown.
Through the criminal thumb-prints of soot, in the swaddling
bands of a shroud,
I pace the familiar street, and the wall repeats my pace,
Alone in the blown-up-city, lost in a bird-voiced crowd
Murdered where shattering breakers at your pillow's head
leaves lace.

1. The Uplands Cinema, now Lloyds Bank.
2. Alfred Janes in his studio over the Grosvenor Flower Shop in College Street.
3. Dylan Thomas.

86. Watkins, Vernon. From 'The Broken Sea,' in 'The Lamp and the Veil,' Faber & Faber, 1945. p.44.

THE NEED OF THE ARTIST

Why is it that, since the beginning or middle of the thirties, Swansea has been so strong and sensitive a nerve-centre of artistic life? There is a bond between all the arts: of this I am deeply conscious. And there is a bond between all artists, of which I am deeply conscious, too. An artist is a man born with a need. This need is so urgent that it makes all his activities return to it, as a centre. The need is always accompanied by a gift, and the gift compels the artist to concentrate on it all his energy and attention. The demands of the imagination must be met: that is the need, and it is always in movement. An artist, then, is someone whose life is incomplete and who is destined to complete it by his art. Does this incompleteness apply to society, does it apply to a town? The artist needs his art, but does the town need the artist? Why put the question? A town without art is a dead town. A country aware of art is a living country.

87. Watkins, Vernon: The need of the artist, from 'The Listener' November 8, 1962.

SWANSEA'S GREATEST POET

In my craft or sullen art
Exercised in the still night
When only the moon rages
And the lovers lie abed
With all their grief in their arms,
I labour by singing light
Not for ambition or bread
Or the strut and trade of charms
On the ivory stages
But for the common wages
Of their most secret heart.
Not for the proud man apart
From the raging moon I write
On these spindrift pages
Nor for the towering dead
With their nightingales and psalms
But for the lovers, their arms
Round the griefs of the ages,
Who pay no praise or wages
Nor heed my craft or art.

88. Thomas, Dylan: In: Collected Poems, J. Dent & Sons, 1952, p. 128.

ABERTAWE

Mae Abertawe yn yr haul
Yn cysgu'n dawel ger y lli
Mae traeth o aur o gylch ei thraed
A Browyr wrth ei hystlys hi,
Caed a fynno'r
Tyrau marmor
Abertawe i mi.

Fe ŵyr holl wamal longau'r lli
Fod iddynt yma wely clyd,
Cysgod ac angorfa saff
Er hwylio o bellterau byd,

Mae pob llanw
Yma'n bwrw
Ei drysorau drud.

Goludoedd prid y coffrau cudd
A ddaw yma'n llwythi llawn,
Olew Persia, mwnai Sbaen
A chnwd gwinllannoedd Groeg a'i grawn
Rhadau tirion
Tyre a Sidon
Ar bob llaw a gawn.

89. Williams, J. Crwys

REQUIEM:

CLADDU'R BARDD O GARIAD

Minnau mewn bedd a gleddir
Ymysg dail a maswgoed ir,
Fy arwyl o fedw irion
Yfory gaf dan frig onn;
Amdo wenwisg amdanaf
Lliain hoyw o feillion haf,
Ac ysgrîn i geisio gras,
Im o irddail, mawr urddas,
A blodau llwynau yn llen,
Ac elor o wyth gwialen.
Y mae gwylanod y môr
A ddon fil i ddwyn f'elor,
Ac eglwys im o glos hâf
Yn y fanallt, ddyn fwynaf:
A dwy ddelw da i addoli,
Dwy eos dail, dewis di.
Ac yno wrth gae'r gwenith
Allorau brig, a llawr brith,
A Brodyr, ni ŵyr brawdwaith,
Llwydion, a ŵyr Lladin iaith;
Ac organ gwych y gweirgae,

A sain clych mynych y mae;
Ac yno ym medw Gwynedd,
I mi ar bâr y mae'r bedd.

90. Dafydd ap Gwilym. (assumed to be anonymous by Dr. Thomas Parry)
Thomas, David Vaughan: Seven Songs. D. J. Snell. 1923.

CELEBRATION:

ODE TO SWANSEA

Bright town tossed by waves of time to a hill,
Leaning ark of the world, dense-windowed, perched
High on the slope of morning.
Taking fire from the kindling East:
Look where your merchants, traders and builders move
Through your streets, while above your chandler's walls
Herring gulls wheel, and pigeons,
Mocking man and the wheelwright's art.

Prouder cities rise through haze of time,
Yet, unenvious, all men have found is here.
Here is the loitering marvel
Feeding artists with all they know.

There, where sunlight catches a passing sail,
Stretch your shell-brittle sands where children play,
Shielded from hammering dockyards
Launching strange equatorial ships.

Would they know you, could the returning ships
Find the pictured bay of the port they left
Changed by a murmuration,
Stained by ores in a night-hawk's wing?.

Yes. Through changes your myth seems anchored here.
Staked in mud, the forsaken oyster-beds
Loom; and the Mumbles lighthouse
Turns through gales like a sea-bird's egg.

Lundy sets the course of the painted ships.
Fishers dropping nets off the Gower coast
Watch them, where shag and cormorant
Perch like shades on the limestone rocks.

You I know: yet who from a different land
Truly finds the town of a native child
Nurtured under a rainbow
Pitched at last on Mount Pleasant hill?

Stone-runged streets ascending to that crow's nest
Swinging East and West over Swansea Bay
Guard in their walls Cwmdonkin's
Gates of light for a bell to close.

Praise, but do not disturb heaven's dreaming man
Not yet awakened from his sleep of wine.
Pray, while the starry midnight
Broods on Singleton's elms and swans.

91. Watkins, Vernon: Ode to Swansea, in Nimbus, Vol. 3. 1952.

BIBLIOGRAPHY

1. Enderbie, Percy: Cambria Triumphans 1661. p. 225.
2. Giraldus Cambrensis: The Itinerary through Wales, J. M. Dent & Sons, 1908. pp. 67-8, 171-5.
3. Capgrave, John: Chronicle of England, Ed: Hingeston, F.C., pp. 186-7.
4 Henry of Knighton.
5. Griffith, Rev. J.: Western Mail, Cardiff, 1904. pp. 194, 197, 199, 200.
6. Gwaith Lewis Glyn Cothi: Ed: Jones, E. D., Gwasg Prifysgol Cymru, 1953, p. 191.
7. Leland, John: The Itinerary in Wales, Ed: Smith, L. T., George Bell & Sons, London. 1906, pp. 15, 16, 30, 127, 153-6.
8. Davies, Rev. J. D.: Historical Notices of West Gower, part IV., pp. 163-195.
9. Kilvert, Rev. F. C.: Diary. Ed: Plomer, William, Jonathan Cape, Vol.: 2, p. 183.
10. Camden, William: Britain; a Chorographical Description of the most flourishing Kingdomes. Tr.: Holland, Philemon, Bishop & Norton, 1610. p. 646.
11. Richards, Rev. William: Wallography, Obadiah Blagrave, 1682.
12. Goldsmith, Oliver: Life of Beau Nash, Sisley's Ltd., London, pp. 5, 11, 12, 28-9.
13. Wesley, John: Journal, Everyman Edition. Vol. I., p. 198, Vol. II., pp. 145-6, 196, 344-5.
14. Defoe, Daniel: Tour through the whole island of Britain, 1745. See also Everyman Edition, 1932. Vol. II., p. 55.
15. Boswell, James: Life of Johnson. Ed: Hill, G. B., Clarendon Press, pp. 161-174.
16. Johnson, Samuel: Life of Richard Savage, F. Newbery, 1775, pp. 141, 163, 165.
17. Savage, Richard: Works, Stanhope Press, 1807, p. 176.
18. Smollett, Tobias: The Adventures of Roderick Random, Hanson & Co., London, 1790. Vol. I pp. 122-3.
19. Morris, Sir John: Unpublished Notebook. U.C.S. Library.
20. Morris, Robert: Will, Secker 248. Somerset House.
21. As 19.
22. Morris, Sir John: Letters to Earl of Liverpool. Add MSS. B. M. Lib. 38267, f 251, f 289; 38275. f 1322.
23. Skrine, Henry J.: Two Successive Tours through the whole of Wales, Emsley & Brenner, 1798, p. 8.
23. Wilkes, John: Controversial letters, Williams, 1771, pp. 107-9, p. 167.
25. Morris. Robert: Letter of Resignation. Town and Country Magazine, 1770. p. 500.
26. Morris. Robert: Letter to John Wilkes, Add MSS. 30871, f. 40 B. M. Lib.
27. Morris. Robert: Speech to Bill of Rights Society. In: Controversial Letters, Wilkes, John. as 23.
28. Wade, John: Junius: H. G. Bohn, London 1850. Vol. 2. p. 355.
29. Hickey, William: Memoirs 1791-2. Adapted from Ch. V., Ed: Alfred Spencer, Vol. IV, 1925, 59-65.
30. As 19.

31. Wyndham, H. P.: A Tour of Monmouthshire and Wales, G. Wilkie, London. pp. 36-7.
32. Romantic: A Collection of Welsh Tours. Introduction, G. Sael, 1797, p. 134.
33. Clarke, E. D.: A Tour Through the South of England and Wales and part of Ireland. Minerva Press, 1791. pp. 195-202.
34. Pedestrian Traveller: Letters describing a tour through part of Wales, Edwards, Pall Mall, 1797. p. 42.
35. Foster, John: Walter Savage Landor, Chapman and Hall, London, 1869, pp. 2, 77, 132-3.
36. Landor. W. S.: Gebir and other poems, Moxon, London, 1831, p. 380.
37. Lamb Charles: Letter to Landor.
38. As 36.
39. Elwin, Malcolm: Walter Savage Landor, Macmillan & Co., 1941, pp. 36, 48.
40. As 23, pp. 68 et. seq:
41. Warner, Rev. Richard: A second Walk through Wales, 1799, C. Billy, Poultry, London. pp. 360 et seq:
42. Oldisworth, Rev. J.: First Swansea Guide, Z. B. Morris, Swansea. 1802. pp. 6-10, 49, 59. Wales, Baldwin, 1804.
43. Evans, Rev. John: Letter written during a tour through South Wales, Baldwin, 1804, pp. 159, 160, 164, 168.
44. Freeman, E. C., and Gill, E.: Johns, Newport, 1962, pp. 27-8.
45. Nance, E. M.: The Porcelain of Swansea and Nantgarw, Batsford, 1942, pp. 83-4.
46. Ibid.
47. Barber, J. T.: A Tour throughout South Wales and Monmouthshire, 1803, pp. 14-27.
48. Malkin, Benjamin Heath: p. 489.
Cadell, Davies, 1803, pp. 14-27.
49. Hatton,Ann: Poetic Trifles, John Bull, Waterford 1811.
50. Phillips, Richard: Watering and Seabathing Places, London, 1810. p. 413.
51. Rogers. W. C.: Swansea and Glamorgan Calendar. Part II. Vol. III. Swansea Public Library.
52. Rabbe, Felix: Shelley, the man and Poet. Ward & Downey, 1888, Vol. 2, pp. 80-1.
53. The Cambrian: Friday, Oct. 11, 1816.
54. Billingsley, William: Letter to his wife, quoted in Nance, E. M. Batsford, 1942.
55. The Cambrian: February, 1825.
56. Bowdler, Thomas: Memoir of the late John Bowdler, Longman, London, 1825, pp. 298-331.
57. Bowdler, Thomas: The Family Shakespeare, Longman Green, 1859, pp. 301-2.
58. The Cambrian Tourist, 1821.
59. Pedestres and Sir Clavileno Woodenpeg: A Pedestrian Tour, Saunders and Otley, 1836, pp. 346-351.
60. Leigh, Samuel: Guide to South Wales and Monmouthshire, Leigh & Son, London, 1835, pp. 315-6.
61. Guest, Lady Charliotte: Diaries, Murray, pp. 243-4.
62. Williams, T. H. Parry: Islwyn, Gwasg Prifysgol Cymru, 1948,

pp. 39-40.
63. Borrow, George; Wild Wales, Collins, pp. 495-7.
64. Kilvert, Rev. Francis: Diary, Johnathan Cape, Vol. III. pp. 187-8.
65. Havergal, Maria: Frances Ridley Havergal, James Nisbet, 1880, pp. 257, 297.
66. Western Mail: Obituary notice of Miss Dillwyn, Dec. 14, 1935.
67. Dillwyn, E. Amy: Rebecca Rioter, Macmillan, 1880, Vol. I., pp. 5-9.
68. The Cambrian: Wreck of Prinz Adalbert, February 2, 1883.
69. Scott, Clement: The Women of Mumbles Head, Samuel French, 1883.
70. The Red Dragon: Vol. I., Feb-July, 1882, p. 84.
71. Woods, James Chapman: British Association Guide to Swansea. (Ed:) 1883.
72. Woods, James Chapman: A Pageant of Poets, 1931.
73. Thomas, Dylan: James Chapman Woods, in Herald of Wales, April 23, 1932.
74. Thomas, Dylan: Youth calls to Age — as 73.
75. Woods, Mrs. J. C. (Daniel Woodroffe): Tangled Trinities, Heinemann, 1901, pp. 276 and280.
76. Sikes, Wirt: Old South Wales, Sampson Low, 1881 pp. 272-4.
77. Bradley, A. G.: In the March and Borderland of Wales, 1905.
78. Gamwell, S. C.: Poems, Cambrian Office, 1897, p. 21.
79. Ibid.
80. Cambria Daily Leader, October 20, 1914.
81. As 79.
82. Davies, W. H.: Autobiography of a Supertramp. Jonathan Cape, 1908, pp. 228-9.
83. Seccombe, Thomas: Forword to the Last Sheaf.
84. Thomas, Philip Edward: The Last Sheaf, Jonathan Cape, 1928, pp. 151-6.
85. Lewis, J. Saunders and Valentine, Lewis: Why we burnt the Bombing School, Swyddfa a'r Blaid, Carnarfon, pp. 4, 8, 18.
86. Watkins, Vernon: From 'The Broken Sea,' in 'The Lamp and the Veil'. Faber & Faber, 1945. p. 44.
87. Watkins, Vernon: The Need of the Artist, from the Listener, Nov. 8, 1962.
88. Thomas, Dylan: In: Collected Poems, J. Dent & Sons, 1952, p. 128.
89. Williams, J. Crwys: Abertawe.
90. Dafydd ap Gwilym. Music by Thomas, David Vaughan, Seven Songs. D. J. Snell, 1923.
91. Watkins, Vernon: Ode to Swansea, In Nimbus, Vol. 3, 1952.